The Living Lenormand

Reading & Magic with the Cards

About the Author

Eron Mazza, host of the podcast "The Witching hour with Eron Mazza," has been practicing witchcraft for 14 years. They are passionate about accessibility and keeping the craft approachable for who ever seeks it. Eron is also an accomplished Lenormand reader and has read at numerous events & venues. They currently live and serve their community in St. Louis Missouri with their two partners and four dogs.

ERON MAZZA

Foreword by Lee Morgan, author of
The Rag & Bone Man

The Living Lenormand

Reading & Magic
with the Cards

Chicago, IL

Paperback ISBN: 978-1-964537-49-8
Hardcover ISBN: 978-1-964537-68-9
Library of Congress Control Number on file.

Published by:
Crossed Crow Books, LLC
518 Davis St, Suite 205
Evanston, IL 60201
www.crossedcrowbooks.com

Printed in the United States of America.
IBI

Dedication

To my dad, brother, and grandma: thank you for showing me it was more than okay to be weird, to speak my mind, and to live as myself. Your love made room for my magic. To Lee, my brilliant editor: thank you for keeping me grounded, on point, and breathing through the chaos. This book is sharper and truer because of you. And to the great God Hermes, who has guided my feet, opened doors, and carried my words when I couldn't—this is yours as much as mine.

Contents

Foreword

Over time you can develop a habit with a particular form of divination—in my case, the dual use of tarot and a collection casting—and you find yourself forgetting the subtleties of other methods. The divining methods I use have become so natural to me, so instinctual, that along the way, I forgot other divinatory arts up my sleeve. This book jumped into my reading list as a reminder of a something that amounted to a missing part of myself. Eron Mazza's words, that spoke of his own history with the Lenormand card deck, conjured up memories of my own past use of the deck. I found myself in the back of a tent at MONA (Museum of Old and New Art) markets doing readings for passersby. I found myself remembering, all at once, the ease and simplicity of those readings. As if someone other than myself had done them... Later, people would tell me how I predicted their next relationship, job promotion, or relocation in another state or country. I would smile, though the compliments didn't feel like they belonged to me; they belonged instead to The Game of Hope.

The Game of Hope, as some people call reading with the Lenormand, is like a hidden biography for Marie Anne Adelaide Lenormand. Each card whispers something about her view of the world, what was important, and the future. They live on my shrine to Our Lady of Roses, and when I go to them, I also go to Her. Somewhere in that relationship lies Marie, not exactly an emanation of The Rose Queen, but certainly a mercurial pathway to her power. A bookseller, cartomancer, palmist, and necromancer, Marie was a powerful seer that couldn't be called anything else other than enterprising. To me, she represents a member of the Honoured Dead who sit somewhere in the middle, almost, between the Rose Queen and the mercurial Master of Witches. Someone to call on and evoke, via her cards, for the practical concerns of life, such as money, relationships, and career. Today, she even has her own *Assassin's Creed* character!

Accounts of her readings are evocative. She is described as having one "wall eye," or what we would now describe as an outward-facing lazy eye. It was a mark of her eye turned upon the Otherworldly, if ever there was one. She was a showman, someone who knew how to create an atmosphere. "The walls of the room were covered with huge bats, nailed by their wings to the ceiling, stuffed owls, cabalistic signs, skeletons—in short, everything that was likely to impress a weak or superstitious mind. This malignant-looking Hecate had spread out before her several packs of cards, with all kinds of strange figures and ciphers depicted on them," Rees Howell Gronow said of meeting her for a reading. It was impossible not to think of her and her many arts in relation to the MONA markets, known for their dark art, taxidermy, and other oddities.

Reading this book reminded me of the subtle pathways to revivify this art in my own life. The Lenormand cards are direct, as the writer points out, but they are also capable of nuance when taken together in various combinations. Eron Mazza gives careful instructions as to the meaning of certain cards when they appear together, while also making clear that any form of divinatory style is an art as well as a craft. You have to develop a relationship with those cards in particular.

This is part of what stays with me after reading, the realisation that I had let my cards get cold and needed to reestablish the habit of picking them up every day, to talk to them, to remember they are a person in the process of seeing into the threads that weave our fate. Eron Mazza's suggestion that you start off by drawing three cards every day—whilst it sounds simple—is invaluable. Not only does it help to familiarise, or in my case, re-familiarise, with the meanings, but it also has the habit of proving the power of this deck. As I have noticed during this process, small, unexpected things are predicted by the cards each day. A growing faith and relationship with them is key to reading this deck.

Each diviner has a particular form that comes most naturally. For me, it is, as I have said, the mixture of standard tarot with a collection casting, a method that allows both Hard Fate and the wild aspects of happenstance to express themselves together. But as Eron Mazza points out, whilst tarot is more poetic and gives a sense of the inner shape of your experiences and what lies ahead for you, the Lenormand deck is very direct. It has been my pleasure to provide clear and concise readings with this deck in the past. I can only thank Eron and their book for this opportunity to remember my love affair with the Lenormand.

In honour of my deck, but also in honour of the Marie Anne Adelaide Lenormand, I have made a lightly perfumed water that I douse my hands with before handling the cards each day. This is intended as an offering to Marie Lenormand through her deck, and is scented with rose, but also with a touch of the mercurial resins frankincense and benzoin.

— Lee Morgan, 2025
author of *The Rag & Bone Man* and *Sounds of Infinity*

Introduction: How I Discovered the Cards

My relationship with divination began at 25 as another chapter of my life was coming to an end. I had just recently come out of the closet to my family and friends—who all had very deep roots in organized religion—so the reception was chilly at best. My life began as I decided to be authentic with myself and others. A few months later, life found me in a little apartment in midtown Oklahoma City with an appetite to find out who I was. The reality of not being able to find myself in a book of laws and stale morality had been quite a shock. I came to the conclusion that I was responsible for finding out what my role in the universe was, not some guy behind a pulpit.

I came across a copy of *Wicca: A Guide for the Solitary Practitioner* by Scott Cunningham at my at my local bookstore, and to make a long story short, I found myself feeling like I had just woken up from a dream. I became a sponge for all things Witchy. I looked for knowledge anywhere that sold Tarot cards and incense. Eventually, I got to a point where I wanted to try my hand at divination, so I started experimenting with runes, Tarot, and

I Ching, but none of them quite fit. I bounced between Tarot and runes for a while, doing readings for myself and trying to squish and push the meanings into boxes that I would understand. All the while, I felt a voice from deep in my mind saying, "you shouldn't have to force anything to make sense." Each feeling of a "failed attempt" made me question the turn my life had taken.

I was getting pretty discouraged until one day, a dear friend introduced me to a little package of cards with random objects on them: a man on a horse, an anchor, the moon. Every card had a playing card suit in the corner that corresponded to the image on the card. When those cards were gifted to me and placed in my hand, it felt as though I was being introduced to someone or something I had known for all my life but was just meeting for the first time. An alignment took place in my mind, body, and soul. Moving the cards and shuffling them gave me a spark of excitement, the feeling of butterflies in my tummy. It was almost like my hand was shaped to hold this deck of cards.

In spite of this deeply profound experience, this soul connection I had found in these cards, I sat them to the side for a season and moved on with life. I kept them on a shelf until one day, while unpacking boxes after moving from my childhood hometown of Oklahoma City to the St. Louis area, I came upon the card deck again. Finding this item was like seeing an old friend after many years, a spot of familiarity during a very unfamiliar time in my life. I set the cards aside, finished unpacking, and then began to shuffle the cards. They felt good to my hand just as they had originally all that time ago. I kept them out on the coffee table in the living room and I would shuffle them from time to time, pulling a random card and putting it back in the deck, feeling that same sense I did before: the spark of excitement; the feeling that words were flowing inside of me, shapeless but as deep and as old as time. I decided to give some shape to these shapeless words I felt inside of me whenever I worked with these cards. I turned to Google for some basic meanings for the cards and started doing basic drawings for myself once or twice a week.

At first, when I started doing these readings for myself with this newly gained insight I had gleaned from online, I would just feel overwhelmed. I felt this resistance to the interpretations of the readings I was doing for myself, like a lot of the answers I was getting each time seemed inherently negative and heavy. I eventually learned the first lesson about authentic divination: a good system with a good connection will not just tell you what you want to read, it will tell you what you *need* to read for yourself. Lenormand has a knack for showing exactly how much delusion you're harboring or exactly how big your ego is. We will visit the issues of personal bias that can pop up in self-readings and how to confront them later in the book. But once I learned to start working on the things that were brought to my attention, I began to feel a deeper connection to the cards, almost like a deep camaraderie was being built with a new friend. I also noticed that the readings started to resonate a lot deeper. Like a phone connection that had been garbled for so long, only catching a word here and there, suddenly started coming in crystal clear. The biggest obstacle to growth in this path was my own illusions.

Later on, I was informed that there was going to be a psychic fair in a neighboring city at a metaphysical store I knew well and was close friends of the owners. They asked me if I wanted to read cards at the event. At this point, I had been doing private readings for myself quite often and felt quite connected to this card deck and now was my chance to take it public!

The day finally arrived. I sat down at the table nervous as all hell, questioning absolutely everything about my experiences so far with these cards. What if I bomb? What if I blank on a card meaning? But then that alignment I described earlier began to take place. In that moment, I felt like I was right where I needed to be with the tool I needed to have.

I was fortunate at this event to know many people besides just the owners of the store. I was friends with a lot of the readers who were also reading at the event, and quite a few I had not met before. I met a man who was using a set of very specialized dice called "astro dice" and a woman who was using candles and paper to interpret from the pattern that the smoke left on the paper. These moments have really come to help me appreciate and love attending psychic fairs! I was sitting next to a lovely woman with red hair from New Orleans who saw that I was reading Lenormand cards and told me it was very interesting to see someone read in that style, as they had not seen a Lenormand reader in *years.* Needless to say, that sent my apprehension through the roof again, as I was left feeling like I had something to prove for some reason.

As the fair opened and the patrons began to wander in, picking their readers, I vaguely remember my first client was a lady with long black hair. She told me that she was having issues with jealous co-workers and an ex-spouse who filled their kids' heads with negativity against her and kept coming into her house uninvited. I read for her and afterward, she looked at me and said, "that was spot on." After that initial reading, I felt a high I had never experienced before in my life! I was so flooded with adrenaline and excitement I could hardly contain myself. I went to the bathroom at the event and did a little happy dance, I felt like I had connected with an old friend I had never met before and I also had this sense of satisfaction like I had just had a really good meal. It was almost indescribable!

After doing a lot of fairs and personal readings over many years, my technique has grown. I have read at many types of events, not just fairs: at private parties, in grand dining rooms, metal concerts, gay bars, coffee shops. I currently read weekly, sometimes bi-weekly, for a lovely bar here in my neighborhood called the Fortune Teller Bar. Being in a venue like this has given me the opportunity to take this art to the mainstream and has afforded me many other opportunities to share Lenormand with the mainstream world. I have read for local elected officials, musicians, lawyers, artists, educators and even clandestinely for a few folks from a certain branch of organized religion who needed a little guidance. But none of this can compare to those first years when it was just the cards, myself, and the coffee table in my living room.

Divination is not just a gift for those that are born with it; it is an ability that can be taught (to a degree). Will it take more work for some than others? Oh yes. Just like there are people born predisposed to math, science, or sports, some of us are born with a predisposition for divination. Consistency is key. Just like building muscle in the gym, the more you work at it, the stronger it will become. When I was growing up, I was always that kid who was known for what my mom called "hunches." I always tell people at my table, "It could very well be you sitting in my seat one day. Divination skills are very much like a muscle; you have to work it out often to get any results." Hopefully within these pages, I will help you be able to do just that. I want to build your confidence and your knowledge on this amazing form of divination that has been used for ages, from emperors to peasants.

This book isn't just for those who are starting out, it's also for those who are seasoned and looking for some pointers to enhance their technique. This book can also be for someone who is just trying to find their footing in the big wide world of divination, and for the person who is trying to find a slice of familiarity in a sea of uncertainty. So, if I am but a stop on your journey or Lenormand is the direction you're going, get ready, because we are about to begin our walk through my favorite form of divination.

It is my hope that you will find connection with the cards like I did and the feeling of excitement I described earlier after my first reading! This book is my love letter to a system of divination that has seen a rise of popularity in recent years and the story of how I came to know these cards.

It's a commentary on how I've come to see and know the cards. I will combine traditional thoughts and my own, having read solely by this means for many years. But this book is by no means an ultimate authority, as there is not any ultimate authority on anything that is divination at large. There are only guideposts. The only thing I strongly encourage in your journey is that you keep a journal and work with your cards every day, even if it's just giving them a shuffle, talking to them, or pulling a single card.

Chapter One: A History of Lenormand

A Brief History of Lenormand

Since our ancestors dwelt in caves (and even possibly before that), we have been finding ways to communicate with the spirit world and ways for the spirit world to reach out to us. Whether we seek to communicate with the spirits of those who came before us; spirits of the land, sky, and water; or seeking the guidance of various deities, humanity has always found ways to get in touch. Whether it looked like studying the flight path of birds (ornithomancy), cutting open an animal such as a goat or a sheep and reading the entrails (haruspicy, and might I add, yuck!), or even divination by cheese (tyromancy), we have found that the other world can communicate in a means that will best suit the world around us.

Cartomancy came onto the scene in Europe in the thirteenth century, around the same time playing cards were introduced there from Asia and the Middle East. Cards were allegedly first brought to Europe by the Egyptians, and historical evidence of divination via playing cards in those regions dates all the way back to the 1400s. There is a clear pattern: first, the cards would be used in play a game, then, eventually, they begin to hold some divinatory significance. Tarot really didn't really pop up until later in the fourteenth century, and it began life as a normal pack of cards used in Italian card games. It is not currently known how someone put divinatory significance to these games, but Tarot is much better known for its uses in fortune telling than it is as a game in modern times. There was not a card deck that was made exclusively for divinatory purposes, and that didn't even occur until the late eighteenth century with the introduction of the first mass-produced Tarot deck, the Rider-Waite-Smith deck (also known as the Rider-Waite or Waite-Smith deck). The deck was created by author, artist, and member of the Hermetic Order of the Golden Dawn Pamela Coleman Smith, working in conjunction with a fellow member of the same order, author A. E. Waite. William Rider and Son was the first to publish this wildly popular set of cards, and the deck has mostly been called the Rider-Waite deck. The development of the third name of this deck, Waite-Smith, is to correct an issue that was made at the time of the deck's creation that omitted Pamela Coleman Smith's name in the title of the deck, despite her renowned artwork being on every card. Prior to the Waite-Smith deck's creation, divination with cards was treated as just a side dish, not the main course. To this day, the Waite-Smith deck remains one of the most iconic and well-known Tarot decks of all time, spawning hundreds—if not thousands—of variations.

We have always grasped for insight and control of our futures. Ancient generals and kings have sought the help of diviners to foretell the result of a future battle, the business person the fate of their wealth and how they can accumulate more, the farmer the state of the upcoming crops, and, even more commonly, the lovesick person seeking to know if they will find another to give their hearts to. People from across the world in every time have sought the help of the Shaman, Witch, or mystic. Whether they lived deep in the forest, on top of a mountain, or hidden in the heart of a city, questioners traveled to far-flung places hoping to get all these questions answered.

We do the same searching even in our modern times by modern means. Instead of traveling a long way, we can hop on social media and find someone who offers Tarot, runes, or even, yes, Lenormand. Even though the phrasing has changed, the answers we all seek as people are virtually the same. This book, however, is not about the numerous paths to seek the will of the sprits, gods, or our higher selves; it is about just one of many methods which resonated with me the deepest.

Lastly, just for a moment, let's all take a moment to be thankful that haruspicy hasn't experienced a revival! I don't think the local psychic fair would be too fond of it.

Lenormand began its life in Germany with a wealthy man named Johann Kaspar Hechtel (1771–1799). Not a lot is known about Hechtel, except that he owned a brass factory, was possibly a clandestine contributor to various essays on physics, and he had a love for designing parlor games. Talk about being a jack of all trades!

Hechtel's biggest success, the Game of Hope, was likely published after his death, around the year 1800. It was a popular parlor game for many years because of its ease of travel. It could be found whether the traveler was on a train to go visit family, a soldier out in the field, or even in the tavern if they wanted to have a quick game while they were enjoying a pint with their friends. According to an English translation of the original Game of Hope, the cards were laid out in numerical order, and people paid into or received money from a pot, depending on if the image was considered good or bad according to the instructions, until the victor received the whole pot. There was a die that was used to dictate the amount of spaces one could move in a turn, and you could use almost anything small as a token representative of the player. Think of it as a very early version of a certain board game where you can be a thimble or a top hat (and without that annoying person who buys up all the properties!).

The game grew in popularity over its life, but it was still mainly only used as parlor game. Thanks to how easy it was to travel with the game, the Game of Hope made its rounds through Europe. It was especially popular in Johann's native Germany, eventually taking off in France as well. Sets of instructions came in both French and German, and the decks followed suits of either German or French playing cards. Even Swiss playing cards showed up in later sets of the game! Oddly enough, there were also instructions for using the cards for divination, almost like a forerunner to the traditional spread of the Grand Tableau. The point in time when the cards became synonymous with the person whose name it bears is unknown in our modern times, though. I believe this came gradually, as popularity giving readings with these cards outgrew the playing of the Game of Hope. And that wasn't until it found its way into the hands of a certain woman in the French province of Alençon, Normandy.

Marie Anne Lenormand

Speaking of this game's namesake, enter Marie Anne Lenormand. Born in Normandy, France, Mademoiselle Lenormand was orphaned at a very early age and was sent away with her brother and sister to a convent school. I like to imagine she had this game in her luggage to play with her friends after long days, that she read the instructions that were contained in the card game and felt the same way I did once I dove into my journey, having quite the "Eureka" moment. She had found her tool.

Mademoiselle Lenormand developed quite an appetite for the occult in spite of her religious surroundings. She also seemed to have had a knack for psychic abilities, amazing those around her by making predictions about various things around the school. One of these predictions was the removal of the abbess (she got in a bit of trouble for that one!). It was after her education in a convent school that she convinced her stepmother to let her go to Paris, where she learned math and how to be a bookkeeper (which she was also very good at!). She was so good that she started a business of her own: a bookstore at 5 Rue De Tournon, which eventually became the base of operations for her card-reading career.

In Paris, everyone, from the upper crust of society to the crumbs, knew Marie Anne Lenormand. Eventually, she started to make friends in very high places. But that didn't make her profession any more legal at the time. Cartomancy was illegal in Paris under the guise of fraud, and the church fueled propaganda that all fortune tellers were associated with murderers, Witches, and devil-worshipers who celebrated black masses with child sacrifice. A lot of these beliefs were brought on by the actions of another fortune teller named La Voisin, who was involved in numerous murders. Poison was her and her network of poisoners and alleged Witches' weapon of choice, and she was responsible for between 1,000 and 2,500 deaths. She was also involved in a plot to kill the king of France, King Louis XIV. Needless to say, card readers weren't exactly seen as reputable in their communities. Cartomancy remained illegal in France all the way to 1994, when the outdated law was finally repealed. So, a lot of Marie's clients came to see her in disguise to avoid the possibility of arrest and being shamed in the public eye. (Seems like a lot of trouble to go to just to get defrauded!) It seems this law was really only enforced when it was "convenient" or the card reader was getting a little too close for comfort to deep, dark secrets and that made the wrong—and, unfortunately, very powerful—people very uncomfortable.

The Reign of Terror and French Revolution

Lenormand came to prominence during the French Revolution, so, as you can imagine, there were a lot of people eager to know what was going to happen next—especially if they were part of the aristocracy! Mademoiselle Lenormand accurately predicted the death of many members of the royal family who came to see her just before the revolution went into full swing. She also gave readings to many prominent players of the most violent period of the French Revolution, sometimes referred to as the "Reign of Terror." One of those revolutionary leaders, Maximilien Robespierre, frequented Mademoiselle Lenormand, whom she told would suffer a violent death. His violent end took place shortly after his 36th birthday. Later, the newly crowned Empress Josephine of Italy came to see her often, much to the dismay of her husband at the time, Napoleon. He was quoted saying, "Man has need of something wonderful. It is better for him to seek it in religion than in Mademoiselle Lenormand." Napoleon found himself the subject of a few of Mademoiselle Lenormand's predictions, including his divorce from Empress Josephine and his eventual defeat, exile, and death.

Not only did she read for Napoleon and Josephine, she also read for many members of the aristocracy from both London and Paris and, allegedly, Czar Nicholas of Russia! She maintained a lot of these high-profile friendships until her death, but it didn't stop her card readings from landing her in jail a few times. According to historical writings, she was also allegedly involved in a plot attempting to free Marie Antoniette from prison, which landed her in prison herself, where she first met the Empress Josephine! At the time of her imprisonment, Josephine was going by a different name, Marie Josèphe Rose Tascher de La Pagerie, as she was married to her first husband, Alexandre François who was Viscount of Beauharnais, who, like her future second husband, was a high-ranking military officer. She also deeply believed in the power of divination. When she heard that the mysterious Marie Lenormand was sharing a jailhouse at the same time as her, she simply had to get some insight and she proceeded to pass a note to the famous fortune teller asking for such. Lenormand told her that she was going to end up with another military man and would ride with him all the way to the top! That's just what happened, because as history tells us, she married the famous Napoleon! This first encounter was the beginning of a long friendship between the two well-known women. Given Mademoiselle Lenormand's many friends in high places, it's not unlikely that her abilities as a reader influenced policy in the countries whose royals and ruling bodies came to see her.

Writing Career

Mademoiselle Lenormand eventually ended up publishing several books on her career as a card reader. One subject she wrote a lot about was her friend Empress Josephine. Two of her more lengthy titles were about her: *Anniversaire de la mort de l'impératrice Josephine (Anniversary of the Death of Empress Josephine),* which was about the encounters and relationship between Lenormand and the empress, and *Mémoires historiques et secrets de l'impératrice Joséphine, Marie-Rose Tascher-de-la-Pagerie, première épouse de Napoléon Bonaparte (Historical Memoirs and Secrets of Empress Joséphine, Marie-Rose Tascher-de-la-Pagerie, First Wife of Napoleon Bonaparte),* which was a two-volume set that went even more in-depth about the relationship they shared, including secrets and other personal anecdotes that the empress told Mademoiselle Lenormand. In my opinion, this second book is one of her writings that could have landed her in prison one of the many times she found herself there. A lot of her other books were political commentary as much as they were about the occult. One of her later works, *Souvenirs De La Belgique, Cent Jours D'infortunes: Ou Le Procès Mémorable; Avec Des Notes Historiques Et Politiques, Etc. (Memories of Belgium: One Hundred Days of Misfortune, The Memorable Trial, etc.)* spoke of her time in Belgium after the fall of Napoleon, where she ended up in jail on Witchcraft and treason charges. (I might add, for all the times she ended up in prison, I don't believe she ever served her full sentence.)

Mademoiselle Lenormand had some odd pre-reading habits she would follow, such as asking the client their first

Notre visitte doit vous étonner?
– Au contraire, ce calcul me l'annonce......

Seb. Le Roy Del. Fr. Janet Sculp.

name and favorite color. Others say it was the first letter of the client's first name, favorite animal, and favorite color. It also appears that she purposely made clients wait a bit before she entered the room and began the reading. No matter how it went, she was renowned for her accuracy. Marie would go on to amass notable wealth and fame before her death. She never had any kids and left all her money and possessions to a nephew who was very religious and burned her occult items (what a waste!) but was quick to pocket the money.

Mademoiselle Marie Anne Lenormand was one of the greatest cartomancers to ever live, whose influence on divination extends beyond the city of lights into the world, even today. She made believers out of many skeptics and touched many lives with her books, divinations, and political influence. Her influence was so great that the cards of the Game of Hope become commonly referred to as "Lenormand cards" around the world. A lot of her books are difficult to find in English. If you're interested in reading her work, I'd recommend just buying electronic versions and using translation applications, most of which can be found for free online. It always adds a bit more *oomph* to one's practice to know those figures who created it and formed it into what it is today.

You can still find Mademoiselle Lenormand's grave in Paris today. Her bookstore at 5 Rue De Tournon no longer stands, which I believe was also a victim of her overly religious nephew's antics. But what you've seen here is an example of how almost all divination tools came from mundane beginnings. She was, and still is, a controversial and potent figure from French and occult history. If not for her, occultism and fortune telling the world over would look nothing like it looks today!

Lenormand vs. Tarot

Tarot started life in Italy around the 1440s as an Italian card game played by the wealthy and evolved into one of (if not the most) popular system of fortune telling cards you find today. The name *Tarot* as we know it today was derived from the Italian word *Trionfi*, which means "trumps." Early Tarot decks originally only had twenty-one trump cards, the Fool being added in the late 1400s, and were played as a card game. Then, Tarot became known by the name *Tarocchi* around Italy, while it took hold with different names in various other parts of Europe. For example, in France, it took on the name *taraux*, and in Germany it was known as *Tarock*. Like Lenormand's beginnings as the Game of Hope, Tarot has been used longer as a card game over the span of its life then it has a divination tool, as the earliest decks were made to be played as a game; it was also a status symbol, because the earliest Italian decks were very expensive and very opulent. The meaning of the Major Arcana has even changed over the centuries. Originally, the Major Arcana was just a reflection of the Italian royal court's daily life, but over time, it has changed to become a reflection of the soul's journey over the course of life.

As far as divination systems go, Lenormand arrived rather late in the game with the Game of Hope not appearing on the scene until the early 1800s, while the other well-known cartomancy system, Tarot, has card decks that have existed since the 1400s (and some possibly even older than that). Their age isn't the only difference. Lenormand has thirty-six cards, Tarot has seventy-eight cards and was based heavily on Italian playing cards, which contain suits of cups, wands, discs, and swords. Unlike Lenormand, Tarot wasn't used exclusively used in fortunetelling until the late 1900s, whereas Lenormand, even when it was called the Game of Hope, had instructions for divination use (meaning that Lenormand has been a divination tool longer than Tarot).

In my experience, I find Tarot has the ability to go very deep with its imagery and symbolism, and can tend to give very cryptic answers to questions. It tends to paint the picture of the answer you seek in very beautiful prose. I find Tarot to be a very good tool of self-reflection, to the point that there have even been psychological studies done about the imagery of the Tarot as it relates to the subconscious, the most famous being by Swiss psychiatrist Carl Jung. This form of divination also has a lot more visibility and popularity than Lenormand, and can be found in numerous books, movies, and television shows the world over.

Lenormand has a tendency to be very "to the point." I saw a good meme of this on social media that asked someone who read cards why they had a lot of different versions of the same type of card deck thinking they all said the same thing, and the answer was pretty spot on about the whole Lenormand vs. Tarot, in terms of vibes. It said, "Well no, it depends on whether I want to be slapped in the face with my own stupidity or if I want my stupidity calmly handed to me with a pat on the back." In my experience, Lenormand tends to do the former rather than the latter.

Tarot is usually the entry point for 99% of people dipping their toes into the divination pool for the first time, myself included. The very first card deck I bought was a Lord of the Rings Tarot deck from a friend of mine's metaphysical store. What made it really cool was that it came with instructions on not only how to use them to read fortunes, but also how to play with them as playing cards!

Tarot also enjoys diversity in the imagery it displays. There are numerous versions of Tarot decks that range from decks based on historical periods to cartoons or your favorite movie (like my favorite Lord of the Rings deck). For the most part, Tarot decks do not deviate from the list of seventy-eight cards, such as the Fool, Hanged Man, Devil, and Death, and the other cards of the Major Arcana, and the Minor Arcana and its suits are pretty set in stone. I have seen some card decks change the names of some of the suits for the sake of the decks theme; for example, I once saw a Universal monsters deck use claws instead of swords, candles instead of wands, crypts instead of cups, and castles instead of pentacles. In my opinion, there is room for a bit of creativity in original card design; at the same time, stray too far and the basic meaning of the card can be lost. Lenormand and its imagery is just as static. You can only depict a scythe, ship, and anchor in so many ways. You can dress them up however you'd like, but the terms and names will always be the same. I've noticed a lot more of the modern Lenormand decks are adding extra cards to their decks. I'll be honest: I am definitely a purist whenever it comes to my cards. Tarot even has two iconic decks still in circulation today, the aforementioned Waite-Smith deck and Aleister

Crowley's Thoth deck. The Thoth deck took a few liberties with the names on the cards, mainly renaming the Strength card Lust, Justice to Adjustment, Temperance changed to Art, and swapped out the page in all the suits for princesses of those suits, but kept the meanings the same.

Now, let's talk about spreads for those two cartomancy systems. Tarot has a well-known spread that I am sure you are aware of called the Celtic Cross, but this is just one of many configurations that Tarot has. There are spreads that deal with everything from what direction your love life is taking to what the road to success looks like for you. Lenormand can be used for these things as well, but there are few "official" spreads, besides the Grand Tableau, that are really well-known. At the same time, this brings a feeling that one has the liberty to create their own spreads. Tarot seems to have a lot more established whenever it comes to spreads and meanings of cards, thanks to the years of history and literature on the subject. This is by no means saying that one system is better than another system, though. Lenormand is not superior to Tarot, or vice versa. It all comes down to what I mentioned in the introduction of this book: finding the tool that fits and resonates with *you*.

As I said earlier, Tarot tends to be mostly allegorical, and Lenormand can be very literal. Let's use a reading that has to do with making money to illustrate an example between the two. Tarot may say that the key to finding satisfaction with money comes from doing what makes you happy, or that your soul must prosper in order for your financial life to prosper. Meanwhile, Lenormand says these are the situations or relationships that have or are currently holding you back from letting the cash flow in your life, whether it is from your employer not being honest when it comes to paychecks, or what you can do to get noticed and get that promotion (or the people and obstacles that are holding you back). Maybe it would even tell you that it's time to push into that side hustle that will eventually turn into a prosperous full-time gig.

Does this mean that Tarot can't give you a direct answer or that Lenormand can't give an allegorical answer to a question? Absolutely not! Spirit will get you the answers you need in the best way for you to understand it, whether you read Lenormand or Tarot or clouds in the sky.

Lenormand in the Modern Day

One remarkable thing about Lenormand I have noticed in recent years is the uptick in readers who have taken to learning Lenormand in conjunction with other cartomancy systems. Something I have seen—and tried myself—is mixing Tarot and Lenormand to get a more balanced reading. The meaning of both sets of cards remain the same, but they complement one another. I have even seen Lenormand decks made by artists that are made to correspond with a Tarot deck made by the same artist. New decks, as I mentioned earlier, may even include cards as a way to expand on meanings and give the user of that deck a deeper or detailed reading, but the imagery of the cards remains the same, along with the meaning behind him, which goes to show how timeless this system is. The Scythe can mean something completely different for the modern reader, but it still fundamentally has the same function. Meanings can be literal and allegorical simultaneously, depending on what you discern from Spirit and the cards that fall around it. What I have come to notice about Lenormand over the years is that it tends to be taken a bit more literally than Tarot. A friend of mine once said Tarot paints beautiful pictures in many different colors and shades, and Lenormand makes an equally beautiful picture, but in black and white, like a very detailed charcoal sketch or pencil drawing.

Another way I see Lenormand expanding is that it is being used outside of just divination is its use in spellwork for us Witchy types! We'll dive into this more in a later chapter.

Chapter Two: Lenormand Unveiled

Overview of the Cards

What follows in this chapter is a brief overview of the cards and insights into the symbolism I have gained over the years. If you are a seasoned reader, you will notice that some cards which are "traditionally" exclusively negative have taken a different context from my years of practice. That's how it's always been with Lenormand: the cards' negativity can be affected by the cards that fall around them. They flow into each other, affecting each other—even the "bad" ones. One of the things I am sure will stand out to you is that, unlike Tarot, Lenormand does not have reversals. There also aren't a ton of fancy spreads like Tarot, and as I mentioned earlier, there aren't a ton of really established parameters. I feel this gives a lot of room to be creative and I have even created my own spread I use quite often, but we will talk about that later in the book.

As I covered in the beginning of the book, Lenormand is a system of thirty-six cards with images based on the suits found in a deck of playing cards, the four suits tend to relate to different aspects of life: the clubs tend to be the more negative cards, like the Bear, the Snake, and the Tower; the diamonds can pertain to choices in life and finances; the hearts to love matters; and the spades to life's transitions.

1: The Rider (Nine of Hearts)

Usually depicted as a person on a horse, I have seen the Rider symbolized in some decks as a bicycle, a marry-go-round horse, or even, my personal favorite, a naked man on a broom!

Keywords: movement, swift change, or something or external forces bringing change

In the way I have come to understand the Rider, it essentially means there is a change coming to your life pretty damn fast. That promotion you've been looking for is going to happen a lot sooner than expected; the break-up you fear is going to happen sooner than later. This card is a portent that a swift change is going to take place or has already taken place and you are now living with the effects of said sudden swift change. As someone who struggles to deal with change, this card can be pretty unsettling. The main message of this card is "you better start to prepare for a transition to come into your life—and fast." In some instances, I visualize this as a tidal wave rushing toward a coastal town. This card, like all the other cards in Lenormand, can take the vibe of the cards around it, but holds a lot more neutral energy than other cards. If the Rider is falling around good circumstances, the fruit of that work is going to be there pretty quick. If the cards around it are rough, please refer to the tidal wave example I just gave.

2: The Clover (Six of Diamonds)

Almost always depicted as a four-leaf clover in some creative way, this card has traditionally always symbolized good fortune! It also symbolizes that we are the creators of our own luck.

Keywords: luck, manifestation, "you always summon what you serenade"

In my experience, the Clover has always stuck by its traditional meanings. It represents a person or actions that create one's own luck, consciously or unconsciously. For me, luck has always symbolized the sum of a person's actions. It is the fruit of their labor. Do I believe in good luck or bad luck? Yes. Now, if it is sweet or sour, that is the result of the intention that was consciously put out into the universe. Luck doesn't blindly find us, we guide it. In short, to paraphrase what I said above, we always summon what we serenade. So, the Clover continually reminds us to reflect on what we are drawing into our lives with our actions. Is it a serenade for happiness, or will the fruit of our decisions create leave us bitter?

3: The Ship (Ten of Spades)

The Ship is almost always shown as some watercraft. It represents voyages of life, moving from familiar waters to uncharted territory, and a new adventure.

Keywords: changes, leaving something behind, transitions

The Ship represents the changes of life. I've always associated it with leaving a chapter of life behind and moving on to something brand new, whether by choice or sudden circumstance. (Look for the Rider to show up in close proximity!) This card has always gave me a bit of anxiety, as I am very much a creature of habit and change makes me very nervous on a subconscious level. On a conscious level, I see change as a sign that I am still alive, as continued change and growth is something done by someone who is still growing and evolving. When I see this card pop up in a reading, especially in close proximity to cards that reference the future, I always know to prepare for a reset. This card's energy is pretty neutral, and its neutrality takes on the flavor of the cards that fall around it. The change the Ship brings tends to represent change on a bigger scale and holds a lot more permanence than the Rider brings.

4: The House (King of Hearts)

The House card depicts a dwelling of some sort, or a safe space. It could be portrayed as anything from a humble hut to a mansion. One of the major things it depicts to me is a space where you are surrounded by family and familiar faces. Family can be either blood relatives or found family.

Keywords: family (chosen or blood), a piece of real estate, a safe space, somewhere to call your own

The House represents people and situations that are familiar and close to you. It can depict a literal home and, depending on the cards around it, if something was, is, or will happen in your close familiar relationships. For example, if the House card is near cards like the Snake or the Fox, pay attention, because this could mean someone close to you is being dishonest. The House card has also come to be a card that represents the end of a journey and getting to a place to rest. While I was growing up, the term "home" was the spot where I felt seen, heard, and safe. Over the years, home for me has ranged from a beloved bookshop or Witchcraft store to my local gay bar, where a lot of my chosen family can be found at any given time. A house is not always a home; home is not always one static place. It's any space that sees, validates, and restores you. Home is where you're truly loved.

5: The Tree (Seven of Hearts)

The Tree represents growth. It can also represent family connections and generational context. To me, it has also come to represent survival and tenacity (again, depending on the cards that fall around it).

Keywords: growth, steady gain, generational connections, resilience

The Tree has always been a symbol of resilience and strength to me, as well as a representation of the power of patience and slow growth. Patience hasn't always been one of my virtues, and the Tree reminds me to appreciate the moments between the sprouting and the bearing of fruit. Something may look like it is not growing, but what's going on beneath the dirt is the most vital part in the growth of a tree: the growth of a root system, which gives life to the tree and anchors it during storms. The roots of a tree are also what connects it to other plant life in the area as well. The Tree card has always been the symbol of someone whose roots have gone down deep, someone who has survived some storms of the past and hopefully will carry the fruit of those experiences into the present.

6: The Clouds (King of Clubs)

The sixth card in the Lenormand list is the Clouds. Most of the time I find it represents feelings of uncertainty or confusion, as well as depression and melancholy. It can also represent a storm of life.

Keywords: confusion, uncertainty, feelings of being lost, a stormy situation, depression

The Clouds card is almost always depicted as either a cloudy sky or a raging storm, bringing feelings of being lost in a tense situation, a loss of direction, or "having your head in the clouds." The Clouds is definitely one of those cards that lean negative, as it can also come to mean a stormy situation or upheaval in life. The thing I always think about with clouds and the storms that they bring is that clouds roll in, but they can roll right out again. I also find some clouds even have a silver lining, if you look hard enough.

7: The Snake (Queen of Clubs)

The Snake card is almost totally negative in context. It represents toxic people and situations, and the image on the card usually portrays the snake ready to strike, bringing pain and misery to the intended target's life.

Keywords: toxicity, deceitfulness, danger, crooked people, corruption

The Snake card usually represents a person or people who are bad news. There really isn't a positive way to put this card. If there was a "red flag"card in Lenormand, this would be the perfect one. I always see this card in "keep your guard" situations. Sometimes I meet people for the first time and something just seems "off." Nine times out of ten, when I turn to the cards for advice on a situation I am going into and that "off feeling" pops up, this card is bound to make an appearance. I know to kindly bow out of the situation they are involved in.

8: The Coffin (Nine of Diamonds)

The image on this card is relatively simple: a coffin either laying in state at a funeral or draped in a burial shroud. The whole scene on the Coffin depicts an inevitable moment of finality.

Keywords: endings, transformations, transitions, the end of one thing and start of another

The Coffin means that something has, is, or will come to an end, depending on where it falls in the reading. Death can be scary, and sometimes the death of a situation or relationship can be even scarier—but also very much needed so we can grow into ourselves and our power. Death is not just the closing of a door; it is the opening of another. One of the things that scares us the most about death is that we often think when the lid of the coffin closes, that's it. But death is not the end but just a doorway into something new—even the newness of a life that we not only want, but sometimes vitally need.

9: The Flowers or The Bouquet (Queen of Spades)

The Bouquet is a card of achievement. It represents hitting milestones and accolades, and can also come to show celebrations and special occasions. This card is almost always to be taken in a positive context.

Keywords: achievements, milestones, rewards, happiness

To me, the Bouquet doesn't just represent achievement and celebrations of goals in one's professional life; it can also represent those same things in their personal life. The Bouquet can represent finally having boundaries with people, walking away from a negative employment situation, or getting help with an addiction or other mental or physical health issue. It is the card that is all about "finally turning that corner."

10: The Scythe (Jack of Diamonds)

The Scythe represents a fast (and often painful) separation, from either a relationship, job situation or friendship. It's another card that can be pretty scary starting off. It almost always depicts a scythe that was widely used for harvesting on farms back in earlier times and is still used in parts of Europe and Asia.

Keywords: sudden separation, harvest, sharp words, cleaning up the old

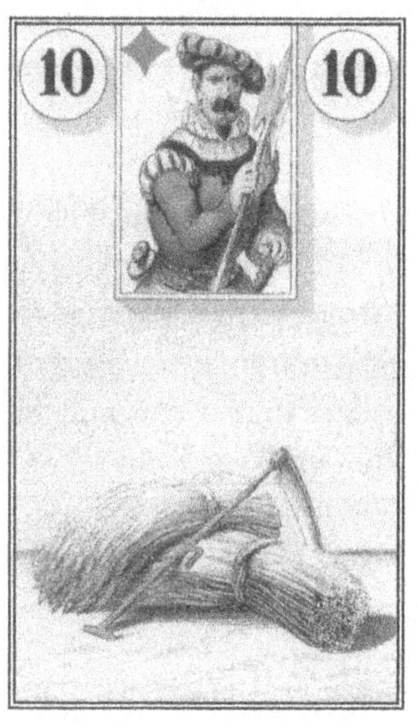

The Scythe can be a card that can either stay negative or be turned around into something beneficial in the long run. Like its agricultural uses, the Scythe can take us away from situations that are familiar and comfortable. Remember, though, just because it's familiar and comfortable doesn't always mean it's good for you. As I said earlier, this card is what you make of it. You can stay down in the dumps after the severing, or you can take the opportunity to build something better. Yes, it may hurt in the moment, but most necessary surgeries and treatments can tend to feel that way, and it's what is best for you in the long run. It's doing away with things that no longer work for you so you can make room for new growth!

11: The Whip (Jack of Clubs)

The Whip is a pretty negative card. It represents pain, affliction, and conflict most of the time, but it can also represent discipline in a new routine.

Keywords: affliction, conflict, discipline, self-sabotage

The Whip usually means that I am being too hard on myself about a situation. I always see the visual of the pious priest whipping himself over perceived sins and wrongs. These perceptions can be given by memories of a verbally or physically abusive relationship or family dynamic. Those thoughts and memories that sabotage and keep us from living life to the fullest that it can be lived. The whip card can serve as a reminder that you are in need of healing. You need to quit beating yourself up over situations someone projected on to you. Don't forget to be nice to yourself!

In a healthy reading, the Whip can symbolize discipline, ordering of your life, and establishing boundaries in professional or personal relationships.

12: The Birds (Seven of Diamonds)

The Birds represents relationships, though it is not as intimate as the House's or Heart's relationships. This card is more about acquaintances and can also represent the office rumor mill.

Keywords: acquaintances, gossip, conversation, advice

Have you ever seen a bunch of birds sitting on a wire squeaking and talking to each other? That is the energy of the Birds card in Lenormand. They are acquaintances, people you work with, or folks you see in passing. They can also represent people spreading gossip or someone giving you advice or trying to have a conversation with you on a particular subject. What cards show up around it will tell you if it's wise to take the advice or not. Sometimes, this card gives me the energy of folks with too much free time on their hands, to the point that they have nothing to do but idle chit chat. The Birds has always served as a reminder to me to be mindful of what I say around folks. Am I speaking with substance? Or am I just turning the wheel at the rumor mill?

13: The Child (Jack of Spades)

The Child card is a card that represents positive aspects of childhood—curiosity, innocence, excitement—but it can also represent more negative things as well, such as immaturity and naivety. The card's art depicts a child or a baby, usually engaged in some kind of activity.

Keywords: new beginnings, innocence, wonderment, playfulness, naivety

When I see the Child card appear in a reading, I always see a new beginning taking place on either a professional or a personal level. It can symbolize going into a new situation with a sense of wonder or other childlike characteristics, or even a bit of naivety or a lack of maturity. It is a very neutral card and reflects the cards that fall around it. The Child can also symbolize the need for us to take time to engage our inner child (at appropriate times) as well. It tells us not to take life too seriously, trust your discernment, and everything will be A-okay.

14: The Fox (Nine of Clubs)

For me, the Fox as an animal has always represented cunning and adaptability. In Lenormand traditionally, it represented a sneaky person or someone of questionable motives. My interpretation of the card is a bit more neutral, depending on the cards that fall around the fox, it can take on its traditional meaning or can represent the qualities I mentioned earlier.

Keywords: adaptability, creativity, cunning, deceitfulness, hidden motives

The Fox is another card that most folks see as completely negative, but I think it can also have a neutral slant. If it shows up in a reading, it can tell you that you are going be in a situation where cleverness, creativity, and adaptability might be needed. I also see the Fox in its more well-known guise as sneaky and deceitful with a hidden agenda. In this case, the Fox is that person who speaks out of one side of their mouth before turning around and saying and or doing the opposite. They promise you the sun, moon, and stars, but it is nothing but words to try and charm you into working with them on their agenda. They are that person that gives you an "off" feeling, and it is for good reason: they aren't being upfront with you.

15: The Bear (Ten of Clubs)

The Bear represents wrestling with issues and obstacles, The card usually depicts a very large and imposing bear in the middle of a forest or road, or tending to her cubs.

Keywords: obstacles, challenges, intimidating, pushy people

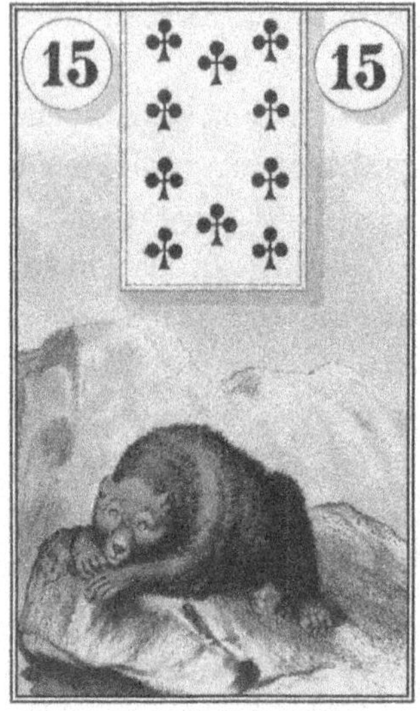

When I see the Bear show up in a reading, most of the time I see it as a time to wrestle challenges of the past, those issues we keep putting to the side and decide to not deal with until they are breaking down our doors or sitting on the path blocking us from achieving our goals and dreams. The more our "bears" are ignored, the bigger and more imposing they can become. These issues need to begin to be worked through, ideally when they are small enough to be made peace with early. Sometimes that is a daily thing for folks, and that's okay! This card has also come to represent someone who can be a bit pushy and try to muscle themselves into your personal space or plans you have. The best way to handle this situation is to set up clear boundaries and to remind them of those boundaries as often as needed.

16: The Stars (Six of Hearts)

The Stars represent the values we live our lives by, those guiding lights that help us make decisions. The card usually depicts one star or a night sky that is full of stars.

Keywords: direction, guiding lights, purpose, values

In early times, ships used to navigate on the oceans by looking up at the starry sky at night. When I see the Stars show up in a reading, I know one of two things: one, I am following the right path in my life, or two, I need to re-evaluate the current path I am traveling. Again, it goes back to the cards that come up around the Star card. For example, if I see the Clouds or the Crossroads near this card, I should reconsider the course of action I am taking. Those lights still metaphorically hold the same purpose for us today, although they represent the values we use to guide ourselves on the ocean of life. Like the sailors of the past, we will be in situations where we lose sight of the stars, and we have to rely on the wisdom of those we trust around us.

17: The Stork (Queen of Hearts)

The Stork is a symbol of rebirth, whether it is here now or that rebirth is coming later. Whereas the Child represents new beginnings revealed, the Stork says, "the best is yet to come."

Keywords: potential, fruits of your labor, results

When I see the Stork "fly" into a reading (see what I did there?), I see changes being birthed into this reality. Your hard work may be paying off or you may be reaping what you sow, for good or for bad. The Stork, more often than not, has always been a symbol of hope. It says the end isn't quite here, but it is about to be birthed into life. I see the Stork has the prequel to Child: the Stork is that hope or dream concealed, the Child is the hope or your wish revealed and birthed into reality.

18: The Dog (Ten of Hearts)

The Dog has also come to symbolize work ethic and the bonds formed in relationships and friendships. It is a symbol of faithfulness and loyalty. They are the friend that always has your back.

Keywords: loyalty, friendship, companion, attentiveness

The Dog showing up in a reading usually has a neutral meaning. For me, it represents someone who has been faithful and loyal in their work or relationships. This card is somebody who has put in the work in. Now, if good came of that or not is revealed in the cards that fall around it. As a reader, seeing this card calls me to be a bit more attentive in matters and "sniff" around because something else is likely happening here that has been hidden. It is the counterpart to the Fox card in that the Dog gives away what the Fox is up to. (I also love this card because I am a big dog lover!)

19: The Tower (Six of Spades)

The Tower card in Lenormand gets a bum rap from its counterpart in Tarot. The Tower in Lenormand can represent a powerful company or government entity, or it can represent someone who is isolating themselves. Every time I am reading for a Tarot reader, I always have to specify, "It means something different in Lenormand!" I always see this card depicting a tall imposing structure from various eras and in various states of disrepair.

Keywords: authority, boundaries, establishment, corporation, isolation

I have always seen the Tower card in Lenormand as a symbol of power, like something made by human hands that people can stop and stare at in awe. But at the same time, depending on the circumstances, the Tower can symbolize times of great loneliness, like in the story of Rapunzel and her long hair. The Tower card usually tells me to either mind my boundaries, because someone is encroaching on my personal space or trying to isolate and monopolize my time, or that I have unintentionally (or intentionally) cut myself off from community and I need to reach out.

20: The Park or The Garden (Eight of Spades)

The Park card, also known as the Garden in some decks, can symbolize social connections, events, or other social gatherings. It is the card of one who has a social life, usually depicting a green space of some type (a beautiful park or lush garden).

Keywords: connection, social gathering, new growth, a place of peace and beauty

The Garden card symbolizes social connections that are a bit more relaxed than the Birds card. I have seen it symbolize new growth from something that one thought was dead, like a garden full of perennials returning year after year. With persistence and dedication, life grows anew. I always see the Garden as a relaxing image and a welcome respite from the chaos of the world. As a somewhat solitary person, spaces like these are some of the most beautiful and most necessary for me to recharge and realign. This card represents that need as well.

21: The Mountain (Eight of Clubs)

The Mountain appears in the distance as a symbol of a difficult journey. It stands as a barrier between you and the summit of your goals. As the Philosopher Lao Zao said, "The journey of a thousand miles begins with a single step."

Keywords: journey, obstacles, difficulty

The Mountain card is a symbol of obstacles coming my way. It shows that I will have to climb uphill to get to the "summit," and reminds me to be kind to myself while I am on this journey. The path to that thing we seek will never ever be a straight line. Sometimes we fall backward and scrape our knees and elbows; this path is crooked and rough and sometimes even dangerous. Remember, slow forward motion is still forward motion. In those slower moments, I feel spirit is calling us to be a bit more "intentional" with our journey. Maybe we just need to slow down, or sometimes we just have to plot a new course forward all together.

22: The Crossroads (Queen of Diamonds)

Across different cultures, the symbol of the crossroads is synonymous with meeting different points. This card can represent the crossroads where worlds meet or, such is represented here, being at a crossroads in life.

Keywords: decision, direction, making a choice

The Crossroads represents a decision that will need to be made. Making choices about our lives at these moments can be pretty fear-inducing for those not prepared. This card's appearance indicates a time to take inventory of my life up to this point and reflect on the distance I have come from. In these moments, I do my research about my options, or I use it as a call to deep discernment and thought. It may call us down a direction we do not want to go, but it is a direction we *need* to go. It may start out a bit rough—allow yourself a season to adjust.

23: The Mice (Seven of Clubs)

These little mice have always been the cause of big alarm. These things certainly are *not* the animated movie mice that help the main character make a dress or do chores. Rather, these are the type of mice that brought plague and can wreak havoc on precious resources. The Mice card represents a gnawing anxiety, a spoiling of profits, or a souring of a relationship.

Keywords: anxiety, destruction, unease, sickness

The Mice showing up in a reading is usually a sign of gnawing anxiety, wasting resources, and disease. It symbolizes the anxiety that can affect the way you make decisions, often leading you to make changes from a place of fear. It symbolizes the spreading of unresolved bitterness that can spread to other areas of your life. To me, this is a big reason to stop and pay attention, ask yourself questions ("why do I feel this way?"), and dig for the roots of your issues. When you are feeling this way, if possible, step back for a moment and attempt to get a bird's-eye view of the situation. Perspective is more often than not needed.

24: The Heart (Jack of Hearts)

The Heart is a card that symbolizes the fire of one's heart. It can symbolize a passion for causes or objects but, more often than not, it represents a very personal and intimate relationship with anything in our lives and all that comes with it, the good and the bad.

Keywords: love, burning passion, intimacy

In my experience, the Heart has always come to symbolize more than just an intimate relationship between people. In some contexts, it can symbolize a cause we are passionate about, be it a job, an art form, or a charitable venture, to name a few. Love and passion can take many shapes and sizes. The beauty of love is that, like Lenormand, there isn't an official way to express it! This card's energy is revealed by the cards around it, and it can get you to pay attention to the areas or people in your life who you do love.

25: The Ring (Ace of Clubs)

The ring has been a symbol of commitment between two people for at least three thousand years. Whether it is a symbol of a marriage or an oath taken, the shape of the ring is meant to show the duration of this commitment.

Keywords: commitment, promise, marriage, contracts

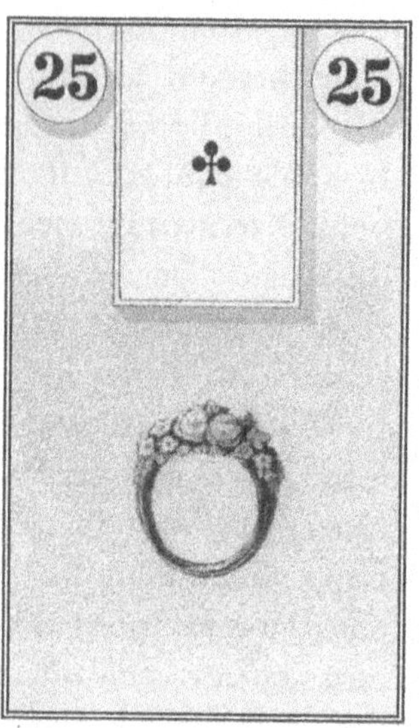

When the Ring shows up in the reading, it can symbolize a lot more than just two people uniting in marriage. It can mean making all kinds of commitments: to a job, a family member, and, of course, it can also very well symbolize making *too* many commitments and spreading yourself too thin. This card calls me to ask myself some questions before I make a promise to someone. "Do I have time for this? Do I have the resources for this? And do I have the emotional real estate for this?" If I answer "no" to any of these things, I know I need to do myself—and the person asking—a favor and say no to that commitment. In spite of the societal pressure to oblige anyone asking a favor or a task of us, especially if they are an authority figure at our jobs or in our families, we do not want to invalidate the commitment to ourselves and our mental, physical, and emotional wellbeing.

26: The Book (Ten of Diamonds)

The Book is the sum of accumulated knowledge. It can also represent a learning experience, either academically or gained by life experience.

Keywords: learning, experiences, school, academia, obtaining knowledge

As an avid book reader, this is one card I can certainly appreciate. The Book can be used for reference or reflection. As a reference tool, it can also be a how-to book for navigating problems you or someone else is facing in their lives. As a tool of reflection, it can also serve as something that prompts you to reflect and appreciate where you've come from and where you are now. The Book is a record to remind you who you are and what your goals are.

27: The Letter (Seven of Spades)

The Letter contains news, good or bad. It can also symbolize a new chapter in your life—or at least the paperwork that is coming for you to fill out that will start it.

Keywords: communication, paperwork, a contract, legal documents

The letter has always been a symbol of paperwork to me. It can also represent communication, via e-mail or otherwise. The letter can represent a contract or legal paperwork. Either way, it is a piece of paper or communication that will begin a new chapter in life.

28: The Man, The Gentleman, or The Masculine (Ace of Hearts)

29: The Woman or The Feminine (Ace of Hearts and Ace of Spades)

Keywords: cisgendered male or female, a masculine or feminine presenting person—whatever you're comfortable with

The Man or Woman showing up in a reading usually indicates a person who presents as masculine or feminine, respectively, but they may not identify as either. I usually refer to these cards as the "person cards." As a genderqueer/ nonbinary person, when I am doing a reading for myself, I usually do not ascribe a gender onto them. The way I look at it is for example, I definitely present as masculine, having a beard and mustache with broad shoulders (and so on), the physical hallmarks society ascribes to masculinity, I would say the Masculine card would fit me, the same is true for the Feminine card. You can actually find card decks with just two "person" cards, which I find perfect for my own readings, considering gender is a spectrum and all.

30: The Lily (King of Spades)

The Lily card is my favorite card in Lenormand. To me, it represents a situation that started out badly but can (or did) transform into something beautiful. As I like to say in reference to this card and the manure used to grow lilies, "This kind of beauty doesn't happen without a lot of bullshit first!"

Keywords: transmutation (negative to positive), virtue, well-earned peace

The Lily card represents a turning of a tide in a situation that didn't start out in your favor. It can also represent peace after a particularly tough situation. This card is the perfect illustration of the ability to take a bad situation and transmute it into something beautiful, and it reminds me to "find the beauty in the bullshit." Some situations make you look a lot harder than others, but there are always traces of hope.

31: The Sun (Ace of Diamonds)

The Sun card represents the dawning of a new day and getting a little light cast on a situation. Similarly, it represents the dawn after a dark night of the soul and the growth that comes with it.

Keywords: dawn, truth, joy, overcoming

The Sun does indeed represent the dawning of a new day, but one trait about the Sun we all have trouble dealing with is when that light is cast on a situation we know isn't good for us. We try to make it make sense to be in those toxic settings, but we just can't find any. I think one of the reasons we have an issue with revealing the truth is, once it's known, it becomes our responsibility to take the next steps, whether it's getting help or getting resources together. The sun shows us the exit, but we have to walk through it ourselves.

32: The Moon (Eight of Hearts)

Whereas the Sun tends to represent more external situations and workings, the Moon represents more internal situations, like emotional, psychic, and mental work.

Keywords: intuition, emotion, rest, mental processes, longing, shadow work

The Moon can symbolize the need for shadow work that needs to be done before you can move on to another chapter in your life. It calls us to work our way through our blockages. It makes me think that I need to step back, look at a situation, and maybe approach it from another angle. Often, our shadow is connected to our emotional state. The Moon is also a very emotional card, and reminds me that it is also healthy to have and feel our emotions, whatever phase we are in.

33: The Key (Eight of Diamonds)

The Key card, much like its physical form, represents an unlocking of doors, as well as a removing of obstacles and doors of opportunity opening.

Keywords: opportunity, unlocking, removing obstacles

The Key in a reading can mean a door of opportunity has opened in your vocational or personal life. It can also mean the opportunity to escape from a negative situation, or that the situation you are dealing with will soon have a solution. Sometimes it can take the shape of an answer we either don't see or do not want to see, and other times we have to go through a situation that is unpleasant to us to get where we need to be: a healthier, safer point.

34: The Fish (King of Diamonds)

I love the Fish card because I find it to be an undeniably positive card. It symbolizes money, prosperity, and vocation, drawing its symbolism from a time when an abundance of fish meant a lot to eat—and a lot to sell.

Keywords: money, job, prosperity, abundance

The Fish card in a reading is a sign of resources. Traditionally, it has always had a lot to do with money, wealth, and vocation. But I also see it as prosperity in your mind and in the soul, which is worth a lot more than any gem, jewel, or currency. Coincidentally, I also notice that those physical things can tend to follow the latter. I am not saying that finding peace will solve all your financial issues, but I am saying that once you put your peace ahead of those things, it's easier to appreciate what you have and it's easier to approach what you desire when you are not 100% focused on the material. You can't put a physical price on peace.

35: The Anchor (Nine of Spades)

The Anchor is a symbol of stability. In everyday uses, anchors keep the ship from being carried away in the myths of a storm or when the crew is at rest. This card represents stability and consistency.

Keywords: stability, consistency, refuge, grounding

When the Anchor makes an appearance, it can be seen as a symbol of being grounded, centered, and focused, unaffected by the ups and downs of life. But I have also seen it as carrying the weight of guilt, unresolved anger, and self-hatred, like you're carrying this heavy anchor around and you know you want to release it so life will begin to even out, but you can't find the edge of the boat to release it over because you are blinded by the same negative things represented by this weight. Once you begin to see those situations for what they *truly* are, you will see it wasn't meant to be carried forever—it was meant to ground you once you let it go. Sometimes, this process is a day-by-day thing that could last for a while, but what matters is that you are dropping anchor.

36: The Cross (Six of Clubs)

The Cross represents trials and tribulations and the taking up of new responsibilities, bearing new burdens. It can also represent resurrection sometimes.

Keywords: trials, tribulations, responsibility, resurrection

The cross is a symbol with a lot of history and energy attached to it, and not all of it good. In ancient times, the cross was a symbol of pain and suffering as it was commonly where people were put to death, but over time it eventually also became a symbol of renewal, thanks to the Christian mythos. To me, the Cross card means going through trials and tribulations, or going through a tough process, and not letting it destroy you. This card is a symbol of growing beyond those limitations and being changed into another version of yourself, putting away the old version of you and beginning the new.

Connecting to the Cards

Relationship to the Cards

The way I have come to understand Lenormand as a reading system over the years is by seeing it as more than *just* a system. I see it as an entity, something with a spirit and personality. It is something you have to build a relationship with, like a new friend or a family member. You can't just meet someone for the first time and expect them to start doing favors. Build a rapport with the spirit of your deck.

The first step to building a relationship with the deck is by seeing it as *more* than just an object. How would you treat an important relationship in your life? Even before the moment I crack that pack open, I start the conversation. I get a feel for the cards, feeling the weight of them in my hand. How do they smell (yes, smell)? Does the imagery on the cards resonate with me? What kind of energy or personality does that deck have? Is it sassy? Is it gentle? Does it even want to work with you in this season...if at all? In my experience, if I don't "connect" with a deck, I don't use it.

Some readers treat the cards as a tool to be used; if that works for them, cool. But the way this path was revealed to me, I was taught to treat them as a spirit with something to say. Treat those cards with respect and they will work with you. Keep them dry; keep them bagged or wrapped. Give them a shuffle from time to time; carry them in your purse, backpack, or pocket. What the cards say to as you divine is a conversation, and if you're reading for a client, what the cards say to them through you, too. Divination is a relationship.

As far as having more than one deck of Lenormand cards, I encourage it. Decks of the same cards have different voices. I have numerous decks, and each one has a personality all its own. They all have the same symbolism in the cards with the same meanings, but they say the same words with a different tone. As of time of writing, I have over forty different decks, each one with its own voice. When I say voice, I mean the way the deck gives advice and guidance. I like to say there are some decks who will speak to you like a close, trusted friend, or a counselor, or, my personal favorite, the ones that can be very blunt, like the older waitress at your local diner that smokes two packs a day and calls everyone "hun." They are very direct with no frills but still loving and very practical. Lenormand tends to lean very deep into what I call the fortunetelling aspect of things. If you look at the predictions Mademoiselle Lenormand gave her patrons, she was able to divine marriages, executions, and other things that were, again, very literal and very to-the-point.

In my experience, Lenormand flows like water in a conversation. One portion of the reading flows almost seamlessly into the next. The card at the beginning of the reading will be related to the cards at the end, like a movie storyboard. (I plan on giving some example readings later!)

Before I go any further, I want to offer some words of encouragement and advice. If you are just beginning your journey with Lenormand, or any divination system in general, patience is key. If it is the right fit, you'll find your "voice to speak and eyes to see."

Selecting a Deck

My first exercise for you is to pick your first deck of cards, if you don't already have one (and a new one if you do!). The following exercise is one I have used whenever I am on the market for a new card deck.

Whenever you are ready to take the plunge…

- Go to your favorite metaphysical store or stores and peruse their divination section.
- Focus on how you feel looking at each deck. Is there a "spark" you feel in your stomach?
- When you find one or a few that shine for you, kindly ask the clerk if you can handle the cards or possibly open them (if permitted). Some stores may have deck boxes already open.
- How does it feel in your hand? Does that spark stay in your soul?
- What does the imagery on the cards make you feel? Does it sit right with you?
- Finally, ask the deck if it wants to work with you, do you get a "yes" or an open feeling? Or is there a closed off feeling?
- If you received the "yes" feeling, then that will be your first deck, Congratulations.
- Journal topic: Go into detail about how a "no" response felt from a card deck and how a "yes" response felt. Did the cards say anything in addition?

Once you gel with a deck, the readings will flow, and you'll likely develop a close bond with your first card deck. I keep my very first deck in a very well-worn blue bag that I feel is comfortable for it to be in. Remember, a deck is more than just a tool, it's a spirit.

Lenormand and Other Forms of Divination

Just as when I started out on this path years ago, I had to find a method that resonated with me on a certain level. It's like shopping for shoes: I tried a lot of them on, and when I felt as though the shoes weren't working for me, I kept looking. In that journey, I gained knowledge of various forms of divination, a bit of the lore surrounding them, and the roots from which they came. So, while the journey was long and occasionally frustrating, it wasn't in vain. I was shown how many buckets there are to dip into the well of divination. I also gained valuable friendships with people I consider to be masters in their various divination specialties.

I will also challenge you to dip your toes into these pools by doing a bit of reading on the cultures and backgrounds these divination systems come from, and if possible, get a reading from one of these lovely systems, and do a bit of magic work if you feel so inclined. I will include an exercise or two after each section. Don't forget to write what you find in your journal!

Runes

The first system I want to compare are runes, specifically the Norse runes. This system of divination is very commonly used in modern times with those who are drawn to the Norse pantheon. The runes were in use among Germanic peoples as a writing system before the use of Latin, which was the language of the Church (and another tool used to eradicate indigenous culture of a region). Later, it was more in vogue to use it as the divination system as we see it today.

As runes were generally used as early alphabets, there are various forms that vary from region to region. You'll find a Celtic version and a version called the Younger Futhark (I will let you do this research if you feel so inclined!), but the most popular is the Elder Futhark. According to Norse lore, the Allfather Odin hung from the world tree for a certain amount of time to gain the magic of the Elder Futhark runes. Runes are used in magic to create amulets, talismans, tools and, in ancient times, inscribed on weapons. They can even be combined in something called a bindrune. Like how magic practitioners create sigils for luck, health, protection, and so on, this process combines letters from the runic alphabet for the same means.

The lore and culture surrounding runes is very deep and rich. I personally have never combined Lenormand with the runes, as I am hesitant to combine two different methods from two very distinct cultures and histories. I see them each possessing a different energy and symbolism relevant to the time periods and areas of the world from which they came. I'm not saying you can't, it's just not a process I feel led to venture into.

A side note here: in recent history, the imagery of the runes has been hijacked and used to espouse the filth of "white supremacy." It was used by the fascist regime of Adolf Hitler and is used today by terrorists as decoration on uniforms and various knickknacks. Runes are part of a cultural heritage; willful ignorance and blind hate are not. Quit hiding behind a deep, rich, and beautiful culture. Having said this, if you are interested in reading deeper on the runes, there are authors out there who have captured the beauty of this system and seek to share it with whomever feels drawn to it!

Exercise: Creating a Bindrune

What you'll need:

- Access to the Internet
- A selection of 2–3 runes
- Your journal
- A piece of unlined paper

In this exercise, we will create our very own bindrune. This will require some research on your part to get familiar with the images of the runes (I recommend sticking with the Elder Futhark). Start by having a look at bindrune examples that are shown online. Do some reading on the iconography of the runes, and you'll see they are pictographs, or a symbol used to represent a word or phrase.

Once you have your runes picked out and your intention crystal clear, how do you see them fitting together? Begin drawing the combination of the runes you have selected. Keep your intention in mind at all times while you are creating this and take as long as you need.

Upon completion of your bindrune, you can say a prayer to Odin, the Allfather, thanking him for the runes and asking his blessing on this symbol. You can keep it on your person, inside your journal, or in an important place in your home.

Journal your experience.

Ogham

Ogham, also known as the Celtic tree alphabet, is contemporary to the runes. They developed in very close proximity to each other, as Ogham was used in ancient Celtic traditions. It consists of a series of lines that can appear to be sticking out from a main line on either side, which can either be diagonal or completely horizontal and the number of lines, depending on the letter it is representing.

Ogham is referred to as the Celtic tree alphabet because each pictograph represents trees that were very sacred to the ancient Celts. Just like the runes, people believe it was used as a written language. And, also like the runes, it turned into a system of divination that has seen a renaissance in recent times. I dabbled in Ogham and still have a bit of interest in it. As far as combining them with Lenormand, it would likely be very difficult to add Lenormand to an Ogham reading and vice versa.

One could do a reading with the Celtic tree alphabet, and Lenormand cards could be used to give a bit of clarification in the result. Again, like with Norse runes, we find ourselves with the problem of one system being very ancient and Lenormand quite modern in comparison. At the end of the day, where there is a will, there is a way!

Exercise: Connecting with Ogham's Roots

What you'll need:

- Your journal
- A park or a nature trail
- A small, biodegradable offering to leave

The ancient Celts believed in the sacredness of plant life, and nature in general was extremely important to them. We can see that reflected in the way Ogham was regarded. They were an animistic culture, meaning they were of the belief that all things possess a soul or a consciousness.

In this exercise, I just want you to spend some time in nature, specifically around trees, to connect with the living forms that inspired Ogham. Touch them, lean up against them, connect your soul with theirs. Whatever you feel called to do—but what I want you to do is talk to them, out loud or in your heart. Ask them questions and be still and use your intuition to answer. You may also bring a pendulum to help receive and expound upon answers. When you feel you are done, leave your earth-friendly offering (like nuts, honey, or some fruit) at the base of one of the trees as a "thank you."

Journal your experiences.

Tarot

Here is a system of divination I am fairly certain most of you are familiar with (given we've already talked about it in this book). Most of the folks I do readings for "mess around with" Tarot or have engaged with it at some point in their lives, myself included. I am sure a lot of Tarot readers started out with the iconic Waite-Smith Tarot deck or Aleister Crowley's Thoth deck. The roots of Tarot go all the way back to Italy and, just like Lenormand, started out as a parlor game. For more on the history of Tarot, you can go back to the ending of Chapter One.

I have known people who have used Lenormand simultaneously with Tarot to get a deeper meaning in a Tarot spread. Tarot deep psychological and spiritual imagery, whereas Lenormand tends to be a bit more succinct and to the point. I believe it is easier to merge Tarot and Lenormand together as they are more modern modes of divination than runes and Ogham.

This next exercise is one I want you to try to do more than once. This repetition will add a lot more dimension to your readings when you need it.

Exercise: A Lenormand/Tarot Combo Reading

What you'll need:

- Tarot deck of choice
- Lenormand deck
- Your journal

Start out by shuffling your Tarot deck. Begin to lay the cards out in a line—no need for a specific spread like the Celtic Cross or anything like that—and pull up to five cards. This exercise works best, in my opinion, when you start with a question in mind. Where am I going in life? Will I get that promotion? Will my significant other and I get married? Will I ever find a lover at all? First, see what the Tarot cards have to say. Then, ask the same question of your Lenormand cards. How well do they line up (or don't)?

Journal your experience.

Kipper

Kipper is a divination system that is distinctly German. I like to consider it Lenormand's closest cousin. Whereas Lenormand tends to have cards depicting nouns, such as Man, Woman, Scythe, and Fish, I find Kipper uses adjectives alongside nouns, such as a card that depicts not just a man, but a mature or "good" man, a card called "False Person," and even one called "His Thoughts." So, there are obviously a few differences. Lenormand also started out as a game made by a German man, but as it evolved, it took on more of a French flavor thanks to the skill of Mademoiselle Lenormand. Kipper, however, remained with its German roots. This card deck is not as old as Lenormand, as it came on to the scene in the late 1800s. As far as divination systems go, it is quite young.

A reading from a Kipper deck flows differently than a Lenormand reading. A Kipper deck is a bit more specific with its card descriptions. You'll find some very nuanced cards like "Bad Health" or "Sudden Wealth" or "Rich Man/Woman." Even though there are a few differences, Lenormand and Kipper complement each other quite well in the same way Lenormand and Tarot do.

Exercise: Kipper/Lenormand Elaboration

- A Kipper deck
- Your Lenormand deck
- Your journal

For the following exercise, I want you to do some research on Kipper. Familiarize yourself with the imagery of the cards. See what the imagery of the cards feel like. If possible, find yourself a reasonably priced deck online (it's unlikely to be in your local metaphysical shop). When it arrives, shuffle it. Experiment with it and see if the cards resonate with you.

I would like you to do a Lenormand reading and use the Kipper deck to open up the reading to more details. After you have drawn your Lenormand cards, pick the parts you want more details on, and draw a three Kipper cards to elaborate. For example, did the Man card show up in your Lenormand reading? Then expound on that. Does Kipper tell you if he is a rich man or a poor man? A kind or immature man? Don't forget to journal your results!

Oracle Cards

What I really like—and dislike—about oracle decks is that there is not really a huge emphasis on structure for this type of divination. They come in a multitude of themes and imagery that can fit almost any aesthetic, and there are no set numbers of cards or meanings across decks. I find these types of cards make great clarifier cards for readings. Personally, I use a forty-eight-card oracle deck called the Earthbound Oracle by Andrew Swartz. It depicts various nature scenes and connects them with different aspects of life such as life, death, and the various transitions and circumstances we all face throughout our soul's journey. There are sets of oracle cards that come from a long time ago, and new decks are being released all the time. It is just a matter of finding one that suits you.

Exercise: Finding The Right Oracle Deck

What you'll need:

- Your favorite metaphysical store
- Your journal

This exercise involves taking a field trip to the metaphysical store again, or looking online for an oracle deck to use in your readings. It will look like the process of picking out your first Lenormand deck from the beginning of this book, but it may take you a bit longer as the selection of these types of cards are quite numerous.

As you are going through this process, keep track of what the imagery on the cards evokes. What does the spirit of that card deck say to you, either from your screen or while you're holding it in your hand? What art styles are you most drawn to? Do you prefer bright, colorful cards, or more gothic styles? What about the range of cards and their meanings? Do you prefer simple, smaller decks like Lenormand, or larger, more complex ones like Tarot? It's easy to get overwhelmed with oracle decks, so I recommend only looking at a few at a time.

If you do not find "the one" in the first go, that's okay! Just pick up the search again another time.

Journal your experiences.

I Ching

I Ching is a system of divination that hails from China. The name *I Ching* translates as "Book of Changes," which is the title of the book that created I Ching. This method consists of a series of patterns called *trigrams* that, when combined, make an intricate pattern of hexagrams used to divine, and depending on the arrangement of the pattern made during a reading, could tell you if you what the gods were saying about a particular situation or whether your luck would be bad or good. I Ching was often used to help make moral choices for government officials in ancient China. It is a very venerable divination practice; in fact, it is one of the oldest (and most unique) forms of divination in the world.

Exercise: Throwing Coins with I Ching

What you'll need:

- 3 coins, preferably the same size
- Something to toss them on, such as a towel or a soft fabric of some sort
- Your journal

Sit down in a comfortable spot and spread your towel or other piece of soft fabric in front of you. Come up with a question like you would for any kind of divinatory reading. Cast the three coins onto the soft fabric and look at how they land. Heads are worth three "points," and tails are worth two. Count what this throw has landed. Odd number totals represent a long, unbroken line, and even number totals represent a shorter, broken line. Write this line in your journal, and then cast five more times for a total of six lines.

Once you have all six lines, you can find what that shape represents in the Book of Changes (which is available online). That will give you insight into your question. You can get a general life reading, or you can focus on one particular area. Don't forget to document your experiences

If You Really Think About It...

At the end of the day, all the established divination systems are oracles (as in the oracles people have sought throughout history for their wisdom, not the cards). Systems such as runes, Ogham, Lenormand, and the others listed here are oracles with a lot of longevity, lore, and power built up around them. Their functions all remain the same, though. They help us connect with ourselves and the places, spirits, and people around us. All of these divination systems can speak to us; it's just a matter of finding a form that speaks the language of our souls. I am partial to Lenormand, and I hope at this point you are as well! But even if you decide down the road that Lenormand is not for you, I hope you will not give up on the path of the diviner.

Chapter Three: Setting the Tone for Your Reading

Setting the tone for doing readings is comparable to an athlete preparing to run, dribble, or throw. Where they stretch to warm up and get into the right headspace, it's good for the card reader to do the same before doing a reading. Readings flow a lot easier when your mind is calm and focused, your body relaxed and not tense. Equally important is preparing your space in which to do readings. There are many ways in which to prepare body, mind, and spirit.

Intuition Development

Intuition is that still, small voice that flows from your mind into your heart without hesitation, It's the voice that comes from within when your mind, body, and soul are unified into one. Intuition is an inner voice we all have, but not one everyone always listens to. In a brief moment of thought, it is the voice that cuts through confusion and uncertainty. It is just *knowing*. We just have to learn to recognize it in that moment. Intuition is the voice that helped our ancestors survive and helped them to connect to Spirit that

has led us down the path of innovation and evolution. Over the years, though, that voice has become hidden in the noise of a world that has grown louder and more distracting.

Intuition is also a very important tool for any fortuneteller. Whether you read Tarot, runes, tea leaves, or anything else, intuition is the bridge that connects the spirit of your cards to your conscious mind. This is why fostering a relationship with your cards is very important. One of the best ways to develop your intuition is by learning where to listen to that voice, and one of the best ways to get into that setting is by learning to calm your mind with meditation.

I have met many folks at many events who have told me, "I can't sit long enough to meditate," so I should start this section by telling you a few things meditation is not. One, you do not have to sit in the meditation position you see in magazines and books, sitting criss-cross applesauce on the floor, touching your pointer finger to your thumb. If that were the case, I'd still be on the floor somewhere with my face on a milk carton. Two, it's okay to get distracted by your thoughts. The objective here is not to silence your speaking mind. If a thought breaks through, just let it happen and release it. Like rays from the Sun, let them float away. This will take some time, so don't get discouraged. I like to use the visual of riding in a car for meditation. We are looking out the window. We may focus on something as we are passing by, and it may have your attention for a brief moment, but then we let it go by and focus back within.

There are many forms of meditation, but I'll talk about three of my favorites here.

- **Chair Meditation:** This is my preferred form of meditation. For me, it's easier to sit and focus on taking deep breaths in through your nose. Just focus on how the breath feels as it goes in and out of your body. For me, it is a lot easier to relax in this setting.

- **Candle Meditation:** This meditation is an easy and effective addition to the chair meditation. All you need is a candle. You can use a taper, tea light, or a chime candle. Get comfy in your chair, light your candle, relax your eyes, and just focus on that flame and your breathing.
- **Walking Meditation:** This one is perfect for those who "can't sit still" to meditate. I first encountered this type of meditation when I visited a Buddhist monastery a number of years ago. It is usually done to the sound of an intermittent drumbeat, with the objective to just focus on every step you take. How does the ground feel beneath your feet? What sounds do you hear? You could do another version of this meditation by just going for a walk in the woods, taking in the feeling of the air in your nostrils, the dirt or gravel under your feet, and just listening.

The point of doing this work is not trying to "get" your intuition to talk; the point is learning to listen to it. It is always talking; it just gets lost in the jumble of other voices and images that bombard us on a day-to-day basis. I have found the voice of intuition is quiet but quite strong and only gets stronger the longer you work with it. Once you start to recognize its voice outside of stress, anger, guilt, or anything else negative we are hit with, its voice will become quite easy to recognize. Start out small, meditating about five minutes per session three times a week, and grow a little either weekly or monthly. You can either increase the length of sessions or the number of sessions you do (whichever you're comfortable with).

Eventually, start including your cards into your meditation so you can familiarize yourself with your deck. Just spend time looking at the images on the cards. Shuffle them—how do they feel in your fingers? Ask a simple question and pull a card. Which card was drawn? Does it relate to the question you asked? If not, it's okay, what does it say to you instead? What does it feel like while you are holding them? What personality does the deck have? Do you feel a little spicy? Or calm, cool, and collected? Just because the cards are in the same family does not mean that they will all speak in the same way. The right deck will give you the right message for the right time.

In addition to mediating with the cards, you can sleep with them under your pillow or on your nightstand and carry it with you in your day-to-day life in your backpack or purse or, if it's pocket-sized, in your pocket. I always have a card deck in my bag at all times. The longer you spend with your cards, handle them and work with them, the stronger the connection that is built and the clearer the communication will be.

Another important way to build this relationship, as I touched on a bit earlier, is consistency! You won't achieve much in terms of connecting to the cards if you do not put forth the effort. Will that require sacrifice in other areas of your free time? Yes, it will mean a bit less time on social media, video games, and watching movies on whatever streaming service you prefer. This practice is asking to fill in the free time you would pick to use to fill downtime. You get out of this what you put into it.

Books are also a great resource, especially if you are just starting out down the path of Lenormand. They are really great for setting up a foundation on which to build your practice. The problem is when they become a crutch. The danger is that we become too scared to build onto the foundations these books make and become trapped in our heads. Isn't this *literally* a book on Lenormand? Yes, it absolutely is. But I hope that you will feel the freedom to venture out and build on to the foundations I have laid here. Divination has no dogma.

Breath Work

One of the important aspects of reaching a meditative state is found in the breath. What follows are a few different breathing exercises that I personally use to get myself into an altered headspace for meditation. It is best to do these sitting down, just in case you get lightheaded and are worried about the possibility of falling down. Whether it is on the floor or in a chair, just make sure you're comfy!

Simple Controlled Breath

One of the simplest exercises one can begin with is simply sitting still and paying attention to the sounds, sensations, and smells of the world around you. Take a nice slow, deep breath via your nose. How does it feel when the breath is entering your nostrils? Cold? Warm? What smells are you smelling? Does the air smell sweet or spicy like incense? Can you smell someone cooking in the house? It's about noticing the small things, not obsessing over them.

Visualize yourself letting that breath fill up your body. What does the energy entering your body look like? What color is it? Feel it stretching muscles and let it correct your posture, bringing your back to a straight and upright position.

Hold your breath for no more than a second, then begin to slowly release it through your mouth. When you do this, imagine the energy from your breath descending into the earth as you release. Repeat this breath until your mind seems "quiet." It's okay to still have thoughts, but the goal is to be able to let them pass through, releasing them with each controlled breath.

Seven-fold Breath (or the Little Death Breath)

The seven-fold breath is the technique I use most of the time. Get back into your comfy chair and begin to breathe in for seven seconds, hold for seven seconds, and breathe out for seven seconds. Remember, be mindful of the feeling of the breath entering your nose and of what it feels like to breathe it out through your mouth.

Tree Breathing

This exercise *can* be done standing up, but like I said earlier, sitting down is a lot safer. Begin by standing (or sitting) with your feet resting flat on the floor. Breathe as deeply as you can through your nose and out of your mouth. As you are breathing, imagine your feet growing roots into the earth. With each inhale, see yourself drawing in energy through your feet. How does it feel? Is it cold, or is there a warmth that comes with it? How about color? Is it red? Is it green?

As the energy enters your body, imagine branches beginning to sprout from your shoulders and back. With each exhale, imagine the branches getting bigger and bigger until the very planets and stars are trapped in your branches. Now feel the energy of the sky being absorbed through your branches into your body. What color is it? What does that energy feel like?

Now let the energy of the great below and the great above combine in your body. How do you see the energy now that it has combined? How does it feel to be connected to the universe?

Meditation is a very important and healthy habit to have, not just as a card reader but in general. It can help you deal with the anxiety and stresses that bombard us on a daily basis. It's okay if you have trouble focusing. It doesn't mean you're failing—the fact that you even noticed you're having trouble focusing says you're on the way! The object is not to "kill" or shut up those voices, but to control how much attention you give them.

Cleansing

An important component in doing readings is cleansing your space. If you have been on any New Age, metaphysical, or "Witchy" person's social media, you will see many different methods of cleansing just a room or an entire house. Many people fan the smoke of sage, palo santo, wormwood, or other herbs through their homes to get the energy going in the right direction. You can use those herbs I just mentioned, but please make sure they were ethically sourced, and do a bit of research on the cultures these methods originated from. I am going to name a few other methods for cleansing, plus my own method.

If you can't get away with using incense to cleanse your space, another good and easy-to-find means of cleansing is with the use of water. Water has been used for thousands of years by many different cultures across the world. Salt water or freshwater makes no difference, unless you have a preference. Just be mindful and only splash a little bit of water so you don't destroy things that were not meant to get wet. Some people will say only use water from a river or the ocean or rainwater, but since those things really are not accessible by everyone, water from a tap charged with intention will fit the bill just fine.

But first, let's figure out what a cleansing is supposed to do. Traditionally, cleansing is supposed to sweep away negative energy and spirits from a space, but it is also a means to fill the space back up with the energy and spirits that will, for our purposes, help you with your card reading and magnify the spirit of the deck you are working with. I look at it like my mom having us clean house when I was a kid before guests arrived. You must prepare your space for work with your cards.

Besides the usual process of burning sage and the other various herbs I mentioned earlier, you can utilize other methods and means to cleanse your space, which is especially handy if your living situation really isn't big on burning things that smoke profusely.

You can find room sprays that contain essential oils derived from cleansing herbs, like sage, palo santo, and wormwood. Another well-known method is using an item known as *Florida water*, which can be found in many forms, including soap, room sprays, and various sized bottles of just the water. Florida water has been used in African and Latin diasporic traditions for cleansing, blessings, and attracting wealth and healing. It also smells really good, as it got its start as a gender-neutral perfume sold in New York City in the early 1800s! It can be added to floor washes to serve the double duty of cleaning on a physical and an energetic level. Personally, I use it whenever I am setting up a new altar space or when I am cleaning my altar. I also add a cap of it to my weekly spiritual bath water to help my spiritual cleansing practices. Another simple and budget-friendly way to make a cleansing spray from sea salt and water. Salt has been used for protection and cleansing across numerous centuries and many cultures.

So, we have covered how to prepare the space. Now let's cover how to prepare the self. Preparing your body is important, not just for washing or banishing negative energy but also for shifting your consciousness and opening lines of communication between yourself and the spirits you will be working with. One of the most timeless ways to do a bodily cleansing is by taking a spiritual bath. As I mentioned earlier, I take weekly spiritual bath to wash away the "yuck" I may accumulate over the week. These baths usually contain herbs, oils, bath crystals, and other things to help me cleanse. In my usual practice, I do not pay attention to the time of day, though in some traditions that can also play a big part. For example, in Southern Conjure or Hoodoo, some spiritual baths were taken early in the morning and had a whole process you had to follow to dispose of the water. A word of caution about adding your own ingredients to baths: *make sure* they are skin safe or that you will not have an allergic reaction to any of the ingredients you add. You do not want those to come into contact with any delicate regions of your body. That would be a horrible way to find out about an allergy.

There are numerous ways of conducting bodily cleansing that do not involve a bath, folks. You can use a cleansing incense or asperge yourself with the stalk and leaves of a cleansing herb like basil, sage, or wormwood. (*Asperging* is when you dip something in water then fling it onto something; the Catholics use it as a technique to fling holy water on people or objects). Or you can even take a simple cleansing breath, which comes in handy if you are in a hurry or a pinch! A cleansing breath is nice deep breath you take in, similar to the breathing exercise on page 81, while imagining the negative energy being drawn from all over your body and breathed out when you exhale.

Drawing in "Good" Spirits

Another aspect of preparation for a reading is inviting beneficial spirits into the space. I always make an offering of incense to the good spirits and invite them into my circle.

Involving spirts of place tends to help clear away some of the "static" that can happen and interrupt a reading, and can help make connections to meanings in cards that one might miss. They also just make for a chill environment!

Speaking of spirits, another aspect I add to my readings is making an offering to an appropriate deity. I have worked and honored the god Hermes for a number of years; he also helps with my readings and I use my cards as tool to interact with him. Working with gods, spirits, or other entities tends to add a bit of oomph to readings, but it also takes a bit of effort because you have to work to build that relationship with them. The first step in building that relationship usually involves looking into a pantheon, such as one that you are related to by ancestry. For example, I am of Italian and Greek descent, so as I mentioned, I have found a connection to the god Hermes. If you want to build a relationship with a god, looking into pantheons your ancestors possibly honored is a good place to start. Sometimes, though, we do not know where our ancestry comes from, as a result of adoption, loss of family records, or many other reasons. In this instance, is there a pantheon that seems to draw your attention, waking or in dreams (or both)? If so, seek a connection to that pantheon. It requires some research into the culture it is a part of and the mythologies it is connected to, but it can be accomplished. I usually find forging a relationship with a god of magick and divination is very appropriate for divination purposes (and Hermes is both).

But who says the spirits have to be classified as gods or goddesses? Some of us have a very strong connection to ancestral spirits. You either connected with them in life, or they have reached out by some means from the distant past. Ancestors do not have to be of blood relation, either. They can be spirits of close family friends, mentors, or many other forms of connection that one might find in life. Ancestors can also be connected to you by an activity you shared with them, or spirituality that you shared with them. Some of us have stronger connections in that aspect than we do to our family of origin. Sometimes, we do not know who our blood ancestors are, or we do not have a connection with our blood relatives for whatever reason. Chosen family and chosen ancestry are just as valid as blood shared between a group of people. The same rules apply though as working with any spirit, though: you have to work on building that relationship.

You do not have to work with any gods or goddesses general in order to do divination. Sometimes all it takes is having a really strong connection to the card deck you are using. Your relationship to the cards is the only thing that cannot be left out of a reading. Ultimately, you can have relationships with Elementals, fairies, spirits of place, or no additional spirits at all. Divination has no dogma.

My Approach to Cleansings

What follows is the method I have used for many years. If you feel the need to imitate it, I'm flattered. But I also encourage you to develop your own pre-reading rituals.

I do four things. I always cleanse my space by sound, light, and smoke. I also give smoke offerings to Hermes and keep his space nice and tidy.

I've used a consecrated bell, Tibetan singing bowl, or even my own voice by chanting a rhyme to cleanse my space with sound. Sound is a great method to clear away negative energy and unwanted spirits that might adversely affect your card reading.

Sound has been used as a means of cleansing and consecration historically. In Europe, church bells were thought to break the enchantment of fairies and the power of Witches and demons. As I mentioned earlier, even the sound of one's voice can be used to cleanse and raise power. Monks from various cultures have used their voices for thousands of years to make and cleanse sacred spaces.

Another element in my opening ritual is smoke. I use incense smoke to invite helpful spirits of nature, place, and the friendly dead to help me with my readings. In this capacity, it's more of an offering than an agent of banishing. I prefer to use natural herbal incense sticks, my favorites being oud and lavender. I always know when I am on the right track with my cleansing and blessing when I see a face appear in the smoke while I'm working.

I have found the use of light to consecrate my circle rounds it all out as a perfect concluding element. I use light to reveal hidden things and dispel the shadows of the past and the shades of the future, symbolizing direction coming to my path.

The next important pre-reading function is what I call "casting the circle of sound, light, and smoke."

Casting the Circle of Sound, Light, and Smoke

You will need:

- Incense of your choice
- A bell or singing bowl
- A white candle

I begin by facing the direction the Sun is most prominent in at that point of the day. If I'm starting in the morning, I face the east; if it's more towards the end of the day or if the Sun has set, I'll face the west.

Light your candle, then use it to light your incense. Find the location of the sun then hold the incense stick out in front of you and begin to turn in a clockwise motion, saying:

"I cast this circle by smoke,
Helpful spirits only to invoke."

Visualize spirits of light walking in from every direction standing in a circle around you. Repeat this three times. After the third time, hold up the incense and say:

"Hail the breath of spirit."

Take your white candle—it can be a taper or a tea light—face the same direction, and begin slowly turning clockwise, saying:

"I cast this circle by light,
That no shadow from my eyes may hide."

Visualize the whole space you're in filling with light and no shadow or dark spots anywhere around you. Like the previous step, do this in a circle three times. After the third time, say:

"Hail the light of spirit."

Lastly, taking the bell or singing bowl and begin the same process again, turning in a clockwise motion and saying:

"I cast this circle by sound,
That no negativity may be found."

Visualize dark shapes standing up and fleeing the space at the sound of the bell or the singing bowl with each pass. Do this in a circle three times as well, ending with saying:

"Hail the voice, hail the voice, hail the breath of spirit."

Make a five-pointed star in the air. Take a moment to enjoy your time in this circle.

After casting the circle, I make my incense offerings to my spirits. Then, I do what I call "waking up the cards." I make as much space as I can between the cards and hold them over the incense smoke until it flows between the spaces in the cards. Then I say:

"Friends, it's time to do our work, our strange work."

I kiss the deck and begin to shuffle.

I have done this process for years and it has worked well to help me connect with the spirits. It is also very protective as it guards against negative and naughty entities.

I know this all seems lengthy and labor intensive, but as I said before, this is something that has worked for *me.* You can take after me (again, I'd be flattered!), or you can see what works for you and what doesn't. There isn't any incorrect way. If I am doing an impromptu reading, I do not go through this whole process. Usually, a quick prayer to my spirits should suffice. You do what you need to do to get yourself in the right headspace.

Keeping A Divination Journal

One practice that is very important when you're doing your readings is to keep a journal of readings that you do. Consider writing down the date, time of day, what cards are pulled, how you interpreted the cards, when you pulled them, and what the results were. You can be as detailed as you like as long as there is a record of it being done and what the results were. For ages, magical practitioners, prophets, and seers have kept a written record of their predictions and findings from their work. So, I am going to ask you to start keeping a notebook, be it a spiral notebook, a composition book, or even, if you have the money, one of those fancy journals or notebooks you can find online or in a stationery store. I love to use composition notebooks, which can be found rather cheaply at dollar stores, or you can buy multipacks on Amazon. The point is you should keep track of your divinations so you can reflect on them later. Think of it as a book of shadows for your readings.

Asking the Right Questions

One of the most important parts of doing a reading is knowing what questions to ask and how to ask them. The cool thing about forming a question for Lenormand is that once you come to understand the cards, you can get as complex (or simple) as you like. It may require pulling a few more cards, but the answer will be found! Think of framing the questions for the cards like you would if you were asking a person a question. The more details you include, the more detailed of an answer you will get, but by the same token, the more muddled you are about your questions, the more muddled of an answer you will get, if any at all. On a more cautionary (yet funnier) note, it really doesn't help to "omit" details from the cards, because they will call you out on it and give you the answer you don't want to see anyway.

Personal Bias

A bit of advice when it comes to readings: make sure the questions you ask are the answers you're ready to know. More often than not, when we turn to the cards and ask them questions about a situation, the cards are going to tell us everything, including what the root issue of a situation is—especially if it's us! This aspect of reading (and life in general) tends to make folks uncomfortable.

We have to become aware of and acknowledge our personal issues. Remember, divinatory tools are really great for self-reflection. When the cards show you something you should pay attention to or something you need to improve on, it is usually for a good reason and can either help you avoid an issue in the future or keep on the right trajectory with the positive aspects of your reading. The future or the outcome you see showing up in the reading, can change whether you follow the insight offered or not.

Looking at our personal issues can definitely bring some discomfort. It has become all too common in today's culture to simply pass the buck of blame to someone else whenever we act up or are accused of having habits that are less than acceptable. It very well may be true that negative aspects and habits and actions could find their roots in the trauma of the past, but once we become aware of them, then we take responsibility to work our way through them.

This bias could be something you picked up from a traumatic circumstance, such as suffering mental, physical, or emotional abuse, or something that you're predisposed to, such as abusing alcohol or drugs or having anger issues. Those things are awful for sure, but we find clarity in learning to control those things. I am certainly not saying it is simple to do so; I had to come to terms that I dealt with an alcohol addiction and had to come to terms with the fact I have to stay away from alcohol altogether (as of time of writing, I am 256 days sober!). Was it difficult? Yes. Was it worth it to discover aspects of myself and find a road to self-mastery? Very much yes! But does it mean I am perfect? Hell no. Dealing with issues that impact our lives, that we have let do so for a long time, looks like a daily resolution to not let the trauma and bitterness of my past take the wheel of my life. My past doesn't own my life; the current version of myself does. The same can go for you.

An unchecked personal bias will cause you to ignore red flags—not just the ones that show up in the cards, but the red flags that show up in your daily life as well. For this reason, you'll find a lot of readers saying that one should not read for themselves and that they should only seek readings from other readers. This fear of reading for yourself comes from the belief that we will see our own fortunes through rose colored glasses, ignoring on coming trouble. Looking at our personal issues can definitely bring some discomfort, but that will only last for as long as you allow yourself to feel it, and there is power on the other side. Understanding your personal issues will also make you a lot more powerful and receptive to the cards. Yes, it is deep, but sometimes you have to untangle lines of communication to be able to identify your trauma's voice from the voice of the cards and the spirits that are trying to speak through them. Divination is for internal work as much as it is for telling the future. Being able to see things clearly means taking off the face we put on for the world so we can see ourselves better.

Shadow Work

One practice I have found that has helped me see myself clearly is the practice of shadow work. I really went back and forth about including this particular section at all in this book. Shadow work involves not only seeing and acknowledging parts of ourselves that we keep hidden for one reason or another, but also beginning to work a way through them. If this was practiced by more people—beyond card readers, too—I'm certain our world would be a vastly different place. There is a certain freedom that comes when we acknowledge all parts of ourselves and know our limits and our strengths. The goal of doing shadow work is to not kill the parts of ourselves that we find undesirable, but to learn to work with them in a way that builds a better version of ourselves. I will say that the first part usually involves taking a very frank look at your life, failed relationships, the gaslighting you dealt with, and so on, to see what the outcome was. Do you find yourself flying off the handle because you feel like you aren't being acknowledged? How about letting people mistreat you because you are scared of being alone? These are things we have to be honest with ourselves with. We have to ask the questions: why do these things come up?

I will encourage you, if possible, to connect with a licensed mental health provider or even a deeply trusted friend. Sometimes all we need is a sound board to "put it all on the table." Journaling is another great way to get our thoughts out and gives us space to be completely honest and not have to hide any parts of ourselves. I've kept many journals of this nature over the years. You can do this kind of journaling in your divination journal or a separate notebook altogether. Shadow work will be an ongoing practice. I will not talk about it further in this book, but trust me, if you give yourself space to see and love every part of you, it will be worth it.

Beginning to Read

The more you put into this practice, the more that will come out of it. With time and practice, you'll begin to understand and feel how the cards flow. A technique that seems to be universal across different divination systems is doing "daily draws." This looks like pulling one or two cards, stones, die, or whatever your method uses a day. With Lenormand, we will start out with three-card drawings. Three cards will be sufficient to start to establish a narrative of the day or a question you have brought your cards.

One- and Two-Card Readings

One unique thing about Lenormand is that it works best in quantities over two. One- and two-card readings are really non-existent in this system. You really don't know what a sentence means by only seeing one or two words; a sentence is at its best when you can see the entire sentence structure.

You can definitely use one card for meditation, but as far as single or double card readings go, they are not really possible.

Three Card Readings

Once you get comfy with the initial meanings and vibes of the cards, you can start reading three cards at a time. Too many cards right from the start can be confusing when just beginning to read. A good illustration of this concept would be when we first start out learning to speak as kids. We start learning how to speak with one word and grow to more complex sentences and phrases.

I start by reading the cards from left to right. Just like reading a book. I start with the basic meanings of the cards and just let spirit do the rest. Let me give you a few samples of three-card readings to help you familiarize yourself with this layout. Enjoy the ride!

Example Reading One

The way I would come to interpret this reading, especially if it was in reference to relationships in your life with the Moon showing up so close to the Whip, would tell me to quit beating myself up (Whip) mentally and emotionally (Moon) over relationships (Birds). Just relax and let things occur naturally; you shouldn't have to force anything to work.

If it has changed from a relationship founded on love to one operating on obligation, then don't give it as much credence or real estate in your mind.

Looking at the Whip card first, I saw affliction or beating yourself up, then the Moon brought up internal/mental processes, and the Birds represent relationships, so I combined them together to get the basic interpretation above.

In a way, you can look at interpreting a reading as divination Mad Libs! You have three meanings, and you let spirit string them together for you!

Example Reading Two

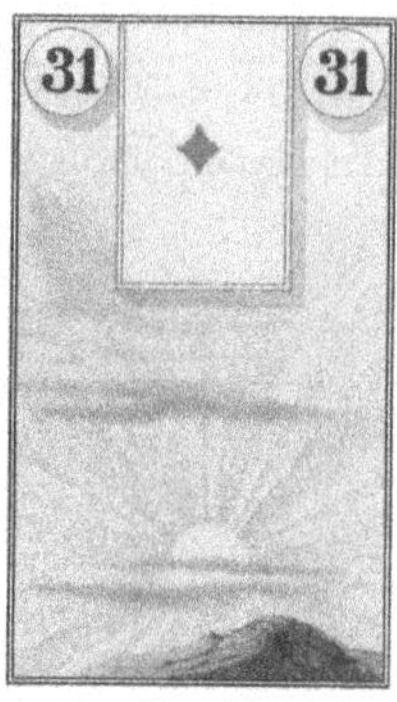

I did this example reading in reference to matters of money. Should one invest money in a friend or loved one's business? Are they trustworthy?

These three cards play well together. They express a positive outcome. But that will only happen if you do some research and get educated, make sure your questions are all answered (the Book) and be faithful and loyal in your obligations (the Dog). The outcome will be a dawning of a new day (the Sun) and a fresh perspective on your finances! Your friend or loved one is being pretty honest with you.

Example Reading Three

I would see this spread as you having to make a decision about where you live or stand. A transient time of indecision in your life is coming to an end, and you'll soon have a place to drop your anchor. Now, whether you like it or not is completely up to you and will be based on how you make your decisions, such as the habits you maintain and the people you are choosing to sow time and energy with. So, what will it be? Wealth or wanting? Follow your discernment!

Example Reading Four

I did this reading in reference to love, as though the person asking the questions (also known as the querent, whether that's you or a client) is seeking romantic companionship.

The Bouquet showing up so close to the Masculine card represents a love who will be charming but also know how to treat a significant other; they will have masculine energy about them and be pretty smart (the Book)! As with all relationships, even when the reading seems favorable, I always trust my judgement when it comes to becoming further involved with someone.

Example Reading Five

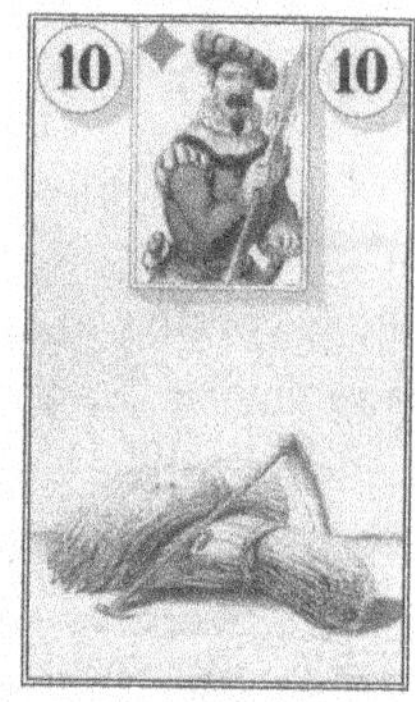

If you are seeking insight into a romantic relationship that isn't feeling good anymore, this combination could definitely resonate. The Whip showing up next to the Rider tells me that one you should not get too attached or move too quickly because this person is a flight risk. The Scythe represents separation, most likely painful, so proceed with great caution. Take things slow and be very observant, for the sake of your heart.

Example Reading Six

The Fish could represent money or a job, but with the Bear making an appearance, the cards say that it will be money that is very hard-earned and will present you with challenging situations. The Letter represents paperwork in this context, like an employment contract or an offer letter. I would definitely either prepare myself for hard work or really weigh the pros and cons of this opportunity.

Example Reading Seven

Starting out this card combination with the Child symbolizes that you are entering into a new situation, like a job or other life event. The Bear, in this context, symbolizes wrestling with big challenges, but what new chapter doesn't have its rough spots in the beginning? Have a little faith in yourself and your ability to deal with adversity whenever it comes up (the Anchor).

One of the reasons I love three-card readings is that it really emphasizes the way Lenormand flows. It tells you the truth in the context of a story. This layout is almost like a sentence, telling you an overview without overwhelming you with too many finer details. It is a great layout for learning the sound of the deck's voice and becoming accustomed to it.

Literal or Metaphorical Meanings

One of the things that sets Lenormand apart from other divination systems is that most of the cards could mean a literal object. In a system like Tarot, there are a lot of metaphorical and allegorical symbols in the cards; in Lenormand, the Letter could serve as more than just an allegorical symbol for communication—it could represent a literal letter. The Man and Woman card could symbolize actual people, who are either the person getting the reading or a literal person in their lives.

But there are also cards that are more symbolic, like the Rider or the Scythe, or even the Sun, Moon, and the Stars cards. I have found it really depends on the cards around them and what you feel the cards are saying to you. For example, let's say you are doing a three-card reading for yourself, and you draw the Scythe, the Ship, and the House. I would think that with these cards, an abrupt change is going to happen and it's going to bring change to your living situation. I highly doubt it would mean that you are going to pull up to your house on a ship wielding a scythe. (Unless you live on an island full of the Amish and you just came from the scythe store. In which case, please tell me about that!)

Or, let's say you draw one of the people cards, the Letter, and the Bouquet. It could mean that someone is admiring you from a distance, or that could literally mean someone is going to send you flowers and a note. It all goes back to how strong the relationship with your cards has become and how much you trust your intuition.

Including Extra Cards

Like I mentioned in the beginning of the book, I have noticed some of the newer decks add cards. I personally don't use them in my readings and definitely prefer to stick to the original thirty-six cards, because I feel like they would just confuse me. (Plus, I've already worked hard all these years to memorize the meaning of the original cards!)

Even though I don't use them personally, I have no qualms with the addition of cards. It is exciting to see this system of divination still growing and evolving. They can add a new dimension to one's readings and display the versatility of Lenormand as a divination system. To me, this is a system that is still evolving and growing. It really makes me view the deck as a living entity. Not to say the other well-known systems are dead, per say, but I guess I have grown a bit biased after all these years! For your first few readings, I would suggest leaving new cards out until you have grown comfy and connected with your cards. But as you grow, if you feel inclined to add them in, then go for it!

All of the cards in Lenormand are related to certain playing cards. You'll notice spades, hearts, clubs, and diamonds on more traditional decks. One question I always get asked is if there is a relationship between the symbol on the card and the suit it is correlated with. I'll say the answer to that question is kind of a "no." Some folks—but not me—will ascribe certain properties to the various suits found in Lenormand, such as diamonds for riches, clubs for career, hearts for love, and spades for negative aspects. I personally believe there is fluidity in the cards. Whether they are conclusively negative or positive is really determined by the cards that fall near them. In short, the suits and the numbers don't really matter a lot to me, as I do not believe the "negative cards" are conclusively and utterly negative. However, I have noticed that one suit that, in my opinion, harbors more negative cards than the others: the clubs. I am not sure of why this is other than just luck of the draw. (See what I did there?)

Other readers I have known use the system of numerology in their readings, which adds another layer of meaning. I feel the same way about this as I do the addition of extra cards. It's not for me, but if it works for you, go for it! Again, I would just stick to the three-card draw I have illustrated here to begin with until the basic imagery becomes more cemented in your mind. Adding too many elements too quickly can be overwhelming and has the potential to intimidate one away from reading Lenormand.

Thirty Days of Three-Card Draws

I am going to give you two different types of homework for this chapter. For the next thirty days, I want you to develop the habit of reading. Do three-card readings for thirty days (at least one a day) about the day ahead, then write about what cards you drew. What are they saying to you? Then, that night, write and reflect on how the reading turned out. Was it a metaphorical prediction or a literal one?

If you feel you are not yet ready for three-card draws, you can do single-card draws and meditate deeper on the meanings of the cards before you begin to do three-card draws, or if you are wanting to do a deeper dive after your thirty days.

For example, if you drew the Scythe, the card represents being separated from things that are not for you, or feeling cut off from a person or a situation, or it can symbolize the term "reaping what you sow." Meditate on what relationships and situations in your life lead to more misery and which situations are more fulfilling. I would also encourage you to meditate on what consequences are going to come of your actions. What seeds am I sowing in life? How can I reap good fruits?

Or if you drew something like the Bear card, you could reflect on what things you are wrestling with in life again and again. What are my areas of strength and how can I apply them to the weaker areas of my life?

Make sure to document your thoughts in your journal, of course!

Chapter Four: Getting Into Intuition!

See What I Did There?

At this point, I am sure you are wondering, "Eron, how do I hone my relationship with my intuition? How do I turn up that voice in my head and turn down the others?" Well, I am glad you asked! Earlier in the book, we covered one way to get into a headspace with meditation. In this chapter, I want to help you cultivate that relationship. I will present some sample readings for you to interpret based on more complicated layouts in order to help you become more confident reading basic layouts. I will also include some real-world anecdotes from my time as a professional reader and discuss how they can relate to one's personal journey.

Awakening the Voice of Intuition

A good (and simplified) definition for *intuition* is that voice or knowing that comes from somewhere deep inside you. It's the voice that tells you when someone or something seems "off," or the feeling of "knowing" what will occur in a situation before it happens. I talk about the way I read being a combination of traditional Lenormand reading techniques and intuition, because real knowledge from the cards is obtained through working with Spirit and the experience and research of those who studied and came before you, but all too often, we lean *too* heavily on book knowledge. Be careful that the knowledge found in those books doesn't turn into some form of dogma you are worried about stepping outside the bounds of. Books (including this one!) are meant to be a foundation and offer guideposts, not the whole of knowledge on the subject. Some of us, as I said earlier, are born with a predisposition to be connected to Spirit. Just like everyone is born with a gift—like in math, art, or sports— some of us are born with a strong connection. Does that disqualify others from divination? *Absolutely not.* It just means that more effort will be necessary. Even if you are born with this "connection," your relationship to Spirit still needs to be honed and developed. It is like a muscle: the more you work it out, the more developed it will be. You get out of this what you put into it.

The thing about that small voice is that it is heard best when we learn to turn down the other distracting voices that can be way louder and a *lot* more distracting. This can be done in a few different ways, but all of them require dedication and discipline to be effective. We also must learn to be able to tell the difference between our intuition and our other competing voices that have every opportunity to scream at us and bombard us on a daily basis. For most (if not all) of us, it will take a bit more effort, because the loudest voice is the voice of anxiety (I speak from experience). I will cover a few different ways that are easy to do a few times a week or daily, in concert with the meditation practice I mentioned earlier to sharpen this voice.

Self-Care

You'll notice the theme among all these different methods is taking time for self-care. Taking time for yourself to just renew your mind, body, and spirit is important in the life of one who does divination. It is important in general, of course, but especially for the one who works with the spirits in any capacity. We are at the best of our abilities whenever we are rested and focused. Being fatigued can throw off your intuition and magnify those interfering voices. If you do not have a self-care regiment, then I suggest you plan one. It can be as simple or as complex as you like. I like to compare self-care to untangling Christmas lights: all the influences we deal with during the day can really leave us feeling tangled up, and self-care is like taking the time to "untangle" and see which ones work and which ones do not.

Journaling

Journaling is perhaps one of the simplest and accessible ways to "detangle" one's mind. I have been a journaler since I was in eighth grade. Writing is a place to temporarily deposit your thoughts, and keeping a journal is like having a silent friend, someone to act as a sounding board for anxieties that build up inside of us. To do this, you'll need nothing more than one of those composition notebooks or a spiral notebook. Like I mentioned earlier, I buy these things in bulk and love to keep them handy. (I love stationery in general, but especially composition books!) I asked you to keep a journal for your card readings (and hopefully you have!), but that could be a good place to pick up this habit. You don't have to compartmentalize your journaling, separating your readings from your everyday life. If anything, we have things like cartomancy and magic *because* we have to deal with real life! Your journal can also be used to keep things that Spirit brings to your attention in your meditations written down as well. Journaling is a wonderful way to keep track of your growth, not as just a reader, but as a person in general. You get to see how your Lenormand journey has helped you to develop and grow!

Here is some homework for you: take a little time each day to journal. It can be done in your Lenormand journal like I was saying, or you can have a journal specifically for your daily thoughts. It does not have to be a large amount of time, only ten minutes or so to start. Do this in tandem with a quick meditation or even just controlled, intentional breathing.

Connecting with Nature

Being in nature is one of my favorite ways to sharpen my connection to my intuition. But how does being outside around nature help with reading cards? I am glad you asked! What better way to ground and connect to every part of you than spending time feeding our souls in nature? All too often as humans living in Western societies, we seem to forget how critical it is to connect with the energy around us. We are also organisms on this planet and maintaining and caring for that connection helps us realize our full potential, not just as readers but as humans. In modern times, we in the West have tried to distance ourselves from our animalistic roots; we have started treating that connection—and nature itself—as more of a luxury than a necessity.

Am I saying we should all still be living deep in caves, way out in the wilderness? Absolutely not. Indulging in modern amenities, Western medicine and technology are, for the most part, there to make our lives easier. But when these start to separate us from an energy and a connection that we were essentially designed for, that is when we forsake a part of ourselves, a piece of our heart. I notice when we find something that makes us feel comfortable and content, we have a tendency to treat nature with neglect.

When a lot of those amenities are outside, we always have access to the plants, trees, water, and wind. Our feet being able to touch grass is our birthright and a necessity. Being able to connect to the spirits of the land, sky, and sea is the reason humanity pushed on to the present day. If you look at the planet, we are currently living in the results of what happens when we, as a species (especially those of us in industrialized nations) begin to neglect this sacred connection. It's not pretty. And I know we definitely need to do better by the spirits that watched us climb out of the caves and into the present. Okay, I will get off my necessary soapbox now!

A good exercise for this practice is fairly simple, and it involves a bit of walking. You will need a place like a park, a hiking trail, or some other place that is very, very "natural." Wherever you go, make sure there is an ample number of trees! Also, make sure you will not be bothered, but not so far out in the woods that you may end up on that milk carton with me! When you have found a good spot, look around at all the trees. Find one that is the biggest and looks the most weathered and, most importantly, gives you permission to work with them. This last point is a pretty easy thing to do. Simply walk up to the tree and ask it (either out loud or in your heart) if it wants to work with you. You will also need to bring an offering or "payment" for the tree that chooses to help you with that exercise. *Make sure* it's environmentally friendly, like fresh fruits, some clean water, or something that can be easily absorbed into the environment if at all possible. If it comes in packaging, make sure that it is biodegradable!

Once you have found your tree of choice, put your hands on the tree's trunk and, either verbally or in your heart, greet the tree and make your intentions clear. Put your hands on the tree. What does the bark feel like? Do you know what the species of the tree is? If not, it's okay! When you are ready, make yourself comfortable by sitting as close to the tree as possible, ideally, the tree will be right up against your back. Feel how grounding this closeness is. Begin to take deep belly breaths and let your mind begin to wander. If you have your cards with you, begin to work with them by either shuffling the cards or simply holding them. What is coming to mind? Some people will think of a question, then pull a single card. If you choose to do that and pull a card, does the deck answer your question? If you choose not to do this, and you just want to sit and meditate, that's okay as well. The point is learning to ground all those other voices in nature.

When you feel you have reached a good stopping point, slowly come back to a waking mindset by counting back from ten, wiggling your fingers and toes, stand up and, again, either verbally or in your heart, thank the tree for the wisdom offered and the peace given. If the offering is liquid, pour it at the base of the tree, or if it's food, sit it either on the roots or right up against the tree. Once you have done this, you have completed the work!

Write in your journal about what you experienced. What thoughts or voices were flowing through your head? What feelings were flowing through your body and spirit? Be as detailed and honest as possible. Does this feel like the "correct" space for you to do this work, or should you look for another spot? Do you feel safe? Did Spirit come to you in any particular form? Write it down!

For the sake of safety, during the times of year when the Sun goes down early or if the weather isn't pleasant, it would be highly recommended to have a "Plan B": a spot in your home.

Setting Up and Maintaining a Sacred Space

Speaking of "a spot in your home" for connection, this is one of my favorites! A great way to build and maintain a relationship with Spirit is to have a space set up for that very purpose. When you are setting up this area, make sure it is a place in your house or some other place that is safe for this work and away from pets or kids. The act of cleaning and maintaining this shrine or altar can help you get into a headspace for card readings or even just for meditation. Should you limit yourself to just working there? No way! This space is for you to recharge, reconnect, and recenter. If your living arrangements do not allow for you to have a whole space set aside for this reason, make sure to choose somewhere that can be turned into an ideal sacred space, like the bedroom, the living room, or a nice candlelit bath. It's okay if the space pulls double duty. My space is currently a small corner in the living room, consisting of a small desk and an incense holder, candle, and various other crystals, symbols, and whatnot. It does not have to be cordoned off.

Light Chores

Once again, I'm sure the connection between housework and your intuition (or spiritual life in general) won't make much sense. The housework I am talking about is not taking care of the tasks that are found on your to-do list; these are the kind of tasks that are part of common home maintenance and are also pretty easy on the body.

Tasks such as sweeping the floor, washing dishes, and folding laundry can help the mind reach the proper state for listening to this still small voice. This is the same method as the one used in the movie *The Karate Kid.* The protagonist had issues trying to understand how he was learning karate by learning how to do chores around Mr. Miyagi's home, such as waxing the car or mowing the lawn, but he finds out in the long run that the motions of these chores are actually showing him the ropes and proper movements for learning karate.

This method reflects the same principle as the sand garden used by Zen Buddhist monks. A sand garden is a large area filled with sand and a few stones of various sizes, in which the monk breaks the sand into fine lines. The repetitive task of raking the sand will produce peace of mind and help with focus. So, any repetitive task, such as the housework mentioned above, would have the same effect, as long as it's not too jarring, loud, or features lots of intense movement.

Ritual

As I explained earlier in the book, another way to make this connection is through the use of ritual. When I say *ritual,* what usually comes to mind for most people is what you usually see portrayed in movies, TV, and books: a clandestine gathering of people either deep in the woods or in a room dimly lit with flickering torches and walls of old gray stone. I, for one, can tell you that rituals like that are really few and far between. Rituals are a lot more than just having an excuse to put on fancy robes, chant, and invoke the "Old Ones." You do a ritual every morning before you go to work or school. The act of brushing your teeth, calming your hair, showering, and so on are all parts of a daily ritual. A ritual can be planned, or it can be done extemporaneously. For our purposes, having a pre-card reading ritual can help you shift your mind and the energy of the space to prepare for card readings.

A ritual, as I stated earlier, can be very helpful in creating a space where Spirit can flow and speak to you clearly, turning down those invasive voices that would try to distract you away from the voice of intuition. A ritual does not have to be long and elaborate at all! So, now I would like you to take steps to create your own pre-card reading ritual. You can use the ritual illustrated earlier on page 90 and follow it word for word, or you can adapt it for your space—or you can create your own.

Rituals do not need to have fancy tools and fancy words to raise the energy that you need. It can be as simple as lighting a candle or some incense with some words of intention, or demarcating a space with a stick of incense or a candle like I do. A good foundation for any work is crystal clear intention.

As far as implements such as incense go, using one derived from something that corresponds to the intention of divination, such as lavender, oud, star anise, or rosemary, is helpful. Do some research, find a scent you like, and let that smoke billow! It doesn't even have to classically correspond to the intention of divination. If it gets you there, it gets you there. Remember, divination has no dogma. Just make sure it smells good so that those around you, pets and people, will appreciate it!

Ritual doesn't have to be fancy and lengthy; it just needs to be meaningful and symbolic of your relationship with Spirit. It can be as simple as a quick prayer or the recitation of your favorite mantra or affirmation. If you have a favorite article of clothing or piece of jewelry you put on before you do spiritual activities, the process of putting it on can serve as a ritual.

Building a relationship with the spirit of the cards, if I have not emphasized it enough, is of the utmost importance for any reader, no matter what medium we use. Without this connection, the means we use to divine are nothing more than objects of paper or stone, like a body without a soul. Another good way to build your relationship with the spirits is by working with them often and getting to know them. It's like making a friend: you can't start a relationship and expect them to immediately start doing big favors for you. First and foremost, you have to be consistent. Despite what we have all come to learn about the term consistency you don't have to interact with them every day at the exact same time, but some time each week should be set aside for meditation, practicing reading, and interacting with your cards. The amount of time you set aside and its duration is up to you, but remember that what you put into this relationship is what you'll get out of it. The "voice" of Spirit that comes from your cards will start to become *a lot* more familiar with time. You'll start to find that that the voice of Spirit will pop up in your daily life and offer you insights, and you'll notice Spirit will also start to take you on some wild side quests.

Story Time!

This story really illustrates one of those unusual occurrences that can take place when we reach a certain point in our relationship with the spirit of the cards. A few months before I wrote this, I was reading for three sisters and a friend who were out for a Saturday afternoon drink. They found themselves at the bar and eventually wound up in my chair. The oldest sister of the three was having her reading, and I got to the portion of the reading where I talk about things that are happening in the present. It looked like they were going through a pretty rough time with the appearance of the Snake and the Scythe showing up in very close proximity to one another.

Then I pulled the Masculine card, and I felt it wasn't a masculine presence that was still living. I said, "it feels like there is a masculine presence that is not on this plane of existence anymore who is walking with you through these negative things you've been facing." I heard a little gasp come from my client, and I asked what happened.

She said, "That's Daddy. I asked him for a sign that he was still around." We all had a little emotional moment, even myself, as my dad had recently passed away. After I picked my jaw up off the floor, we continued with the reading.

This story is a good example of what can be achieved when someone has made a very strong connection with their cards and is a prime example of what you get out of this path when you put the work into it. I am by no means a medium, but with the appearance of cards like the Masculine card and the Coffin showing up in close proximity and a well-developed relationship with my intuition, I sensed that this was an unusual occurrence. Whenever it comes to divination and card readings, it just helps to remain open to whatever Spirit wants to do through your medium of divination. Remember, divination has no dogma.

Tips for Insightful Readings

Confidence is another tool that is right up there in importance with sharpening your intuition. In fact, you can practice all day and night, but if you second guess yourself and your connection to the cards, you will have a very difficult time following the voice of Spirit. When I say *confidence,* I am certainly not talking about showboating showing off that would be called *over-confidence.* The kind I am talking about is the same kind of confidence in one's relationship in your connection, like being confident in the relationship one has with a very dear friend. It is a confidence that they will be there to lend a listening ear and offer words of guidance; confidence and faith that no matter what, your relationship with Spirit will guide you through it.

Complex Card Combinations and Negative Cards

At some point in your divinatory path, you will come across a combination of cards that will absolutely stump you. Cards that seem to be at the opposite ends of the spectrum in terms of being positive or negative, such as a super positive card like the Fish showing up next to (or fairly close to) a card that can seem like "bad news." This can be especially powerful when the spread is smaller, like a three- or five-card spread. The first thing I do is see what Spirit is saying more broadly. If you are having trouble with that, the first thing you should do is take a look at the reading as a whole. We always have to make sure we are not fixating on a single card that can seem super scary. That is like pausing a movie when the main character is at its lowest and never moving on to see how the rest of the story turns out.

Let's use a three-card spread as an example.

The Fox/the Fish/the Stork

When I see the Fox, a card that has traditionally been a symbol of someone that is dishonest and sneaky, so close to a card that symbolizes one's money, it would immediately make me want to put a fraud alert on my bank accounts and credit card and be very suspicious of everyone around me. But instead of taking all your money out of your bank and stuffing it in your mattress, take a look at the card that is rounding out this spread: the Stork, which symbolizes new beginnings, things getting birthed, and thus new things being "born" into this reality. I would come to interpret this as your money will help you bring your dreams about, but the Fox tells you to be discerning with whom you share those dreams with, because not everyone can be trusted. Be wise with your prosperity and with whom you share it with.

What we can draw from this example, as I stated above, is not to fixate on the possibility of *who* the Fox is, just prepare for the Fox's arrival. To quote the old hip-hop adage, "if you stay ready, you don't have to get ready." Don't let the flow of anxiety block out the flow of the spirit. I will talk more about dealing with negative cards on the next page.

Let's do another example, this time in a five-card format.

The Snake/the Tower/the Masculine/the Clover/the Child

I can honestly say I would gasp a little bit at the sight of the Snake, even after fourteen years of reading Lenormand and I'll be honest—I actually do. With the Tower card and Masculine card being so close I would take this to mean to an older masculine person is absolutely out to get me, join the witness protection program and flee the country. But don't do that! You still have two other cards—the Clover and the Child! Remember, pay attention to what the voice of Spirit is saying. If you sometimes have to do your spread and walk away for a bit to really let the voice of Spirit rise back up, then do that. Sometimes, we have to walk the anxiety out and let our minds calm down a bit before going back to the reading and taking a fresh look.

Here is how I would interpret this spread: there is an older masculine person in your life who really does not have the best intentions, and the Clover and the Child are bringing fortune with a new beginning. Don't let that toxic person from your past re-attach themselves and take away the hard-earned fruit of your labor. Share your fortunate news with a privileged few.

Dealing with Negative Cards

One time, I was reading for a couple and something seemed "off" about one partner who was overly eager to sit in on this reading, yet very cold. I begin reading in the same manner as I illustrated above. I couldn't shake the strange feeling. I eventually pulled the Whip, the Snake, and the Man in reference to my client's present situation. I referred to them being around a toxic masculine energy that was really not good for them. It was pretty easy for me to put two and two together, not to mention the guy was burning a hole through me after that with his glare. That man was bad news for his partner and he knew that I knew. I kept going with that reading and eventually ended by telling my client, "Once you get away from that negative presence, your life will start to change."

Fast forward a few months: it was now summer and the gentlemen I read for came back to the Fortune Teller Bar to see me. I gave him his reading and noticed he had just gone through a pretty rough separation from a situation that was not good for him. He looked at me; I looked back at him, and saw emotion splashed across his face. He'd listened to the cards and got out of his abusive relationship.

The best kind of card readers are ones who are not afraid to deal with the rough news along with the good news. The way we deal with the speed bumps of life, and the way we deal with negativity that we are told is going to take place in our lives is a great barometer of how we deal with challenges in general. Not every reading you do is going to be 100% positive 100% of the time. Life happens, bad stuff happens, and when I go see a reader to get some insight on a situation (even a reader needs a reader sometimes!), one of the things I always pay attention to is how the person presents negative aspects, if at all.

One of the biggest problems with reading for ourselves, that I have brought up a few times in this book, is that we have a tendency to defer to personal bias, which generally comes up in two shapes. Personal bias can look like seeing something unflattering popping out in the cards and thinking, "this can't be for me," when, in fact, the reading you're doing is *for you,* and then ignore it. Or it can look and feel like being the "deer in the headlights" and still not doing anything because the reading is perceived as being final and unavoidable.

What we seem to forget is that the future is not set in stone. The future is fluid! The future you see showing up in the cards is not one to be feared; it is simply showing where you'll be if you continue down the path you're on.

As you have noticed, in my example readings is the appearance of negative cards. I promise you will encounter them on your journey as well. It's really nothing to freak out about, as bad stuff happens in life. This is where the whole identifying your personal biases thing can come in handy.

When cards like the Mountain, Snake, Whip, Scythe, and Coffin show up, it can be a pretty scary feeling. But it can also be revealing about how we deal with negativity in our lives. Do we ignore necessary change and are just destined to repeat the same issues? Or do we fixate on it and let it incapacitate us with fear? When I see negative cards pop up in my personal readings, I like to use them as a tool for self-reflection, which, as I stated earlier, is one of the primary functions of divination. I also use it as a "early detection system." When I see that negative card pop up when I am doing my daily reading, whether it is in reference to events of the day or someone I will be meeting, those cards inspire me to dig a bit deeper and take a peek beyond the surface of a situation. If they are referring to rough patches in life that we're going through or will be facing, they can also help us remember the finiteness of those situations. We do not "solve" our negative cards by fixating on them or ignoring them, we handle them by trusting our intuition and by having faith in ourselves. We *will* come out on the other side or be able to change our lives in a positive way that will lessen or eliminate those problems all together.

A Few Words of Advice

Be Real with Yourself

This leads me to the first and best piece of advice I can offer for poignant and powerful readings. Be real with where you are in your life and what you see in the cards. If you see an issue you are currently dealing with show up in the cards and the spirits are trying to show you that you are needing to make a U-turn, then I would take a step back and look at the direction your life is going. The first step to fixing an issue in our lives is to admit there *is* an issue.

Give Your Relationship with Spirit Some Credit!

Have a little faith when it comes to your connection with Spirit and your deck. This point also comes in handy whenever you are interpreting very difficult card combinations. You'll know, even if it seems like an odd combo of cards, trust your intuition. If you have to turn to a book, that is A-okay. Spirit knows that sometimes we can be so close to a situation, we need a refresher or even just a bit of clarification.

When the Reading isn't Resonating

Occasionally you'll do a reading and have cards that don't resonate with you. That's okay! One of two things is taking place here: sometimes we need to dive deeper and strengthen our connections to the deck, or sometimes we need to take a bit of time and just meditate on the combination. Like I've said, trust your intuition: the answer will come.

Another thing I used to run into is when a portion of the reading absolutely connects, but another part really seems like it has come out of left field. It's not uncommon for a part of the reading to be a bit off, but then one part is *bam!*—right on. This means that the Spirit usually wants us to focus on and look into the aspect of the reading that isn't very clear. We are being invited to dig a little deeper into the past that is being shown in the spread, or to investigate a problem. Maybe the answer you're seeking is just below the surface.

You'll usually run into things like this in the portions of your reading referring to the past or present. We can say that about the future as well, but there will be a lack of certainty, as the future hasn't happened yet. As I said earlier, the future is fluid! It could go from something that doesn't connect at all to feeling like we should have listened to the cards.

Starting Small

This is a bit off topic from the rest of the chapter, but something I feel should be brought up. As with all things worthwhile, it's okay to start small when reading Lenormand. It's easy to feel inadequate when you start reading, especially when you hop on social media and see people who have been reading for ages performing complex readings or doing it as their full-time job. I really dealt with feelings of inadequacy when I started out on this journey, and the best way I found to deal with this is to find friendly mentors. People will train and guide you, people who were at the beginning of their journey as you are. More often than not, I have found most readers (myself included) love to talk about their craft.

Wherever you are in your Lenormand journey, enjoy it. Don't worry about other people. Learn from the cards. They tell you what you need to know and they will show you how to grow. Don't be in a such a hurry to "make it to the big time." We don't start down this path looking to make it rich, after all. This path is for those who don't fear the reflection they see in the mirror. Divination is a map and mirror for self-reflection, not a star-maker.

Chapter Five: Diving Deeper: Advanced Layouts and Spreads

Once you start to get into more complex readings, you will really begin to see the connectivity of the cards. It is important, however, to understand what I mean when I say "connectivity of the cards." You can see it in how the card at the beginning of the reading relates to the card at the end. In keeping with the example of writing a sentence, it means understanding how the words (cards) relate to one another. If the words of a sentence do not have anything to do with one another, then you have nothing more than a jumble of confusing words! It's no better than those little word magnets some folks have on their fridge and use to make funny, and more often than not inappropriate, sentences. (Well, at least *I* make funny, inappropriate sentences.)

When I begin to interpret readings, especially more complex ones, I do an initial pass to get the foundation of the reading or the theme. I will then see how the cards influence each other in the reading; this is also easier to intuit with a bigger reading. Three card readings, I find, are good for awakening and beginning to understand the cards and how Spirit

flows through them. It's like beginning to learn to speak a new language; start with simple sentences, then you can move on to more complicated conversations with more details. Again, it's okay to start small!

Let's go through a few examples of how one could interpret a five- or seven-card reading.

Five-Card Example Readings

The Whip/the Snake/the Rider/the House/the Ship

I would read this as a conflict (the Whip) with a toxic person or people (Snake) is going to bring in some drama into your personal life (House). This will bring a swift, fast change (the Rider). Get ahead of it and make some changes and leave people who aren't good for you behind. Move on to a better situation (Ship).

The Fish/the Birds/the Whip/the Scythe/the Ship

People are having heated conversations at work (Fish and Birds), and it will not end very well. There will be layoffs coming (Whip/Scythe) so you should begin to get your resume out in the job market (Ship).

This spread could also be read as issues with co-workers and there are conversations (Fish/Birds) taking place that could make work more difficult and that could result in some painful situations (Whip). It may be best to cut ties (Scythe) then sail into something new (Ship).

The House/the Anchor/the Fish/the Man/the Lilies

I would take this reading positively, especially if I am doing a reading during a very hectic and transitional time in my life. The House and Anchor showing up together tell me that I will be in a new safe space soon, and I'll be able to drop my anchor there. The Fish tells me that the situation will be all the sweeter, as this new era of my life will contain a lot more prosperity of the mind and heart as well as prosperity in a materialistic sense, as the Lilies tell me that all of my hard work and changes being made are going to pay off. I use the Masculine card here to symbolize myself here. To sum it up, the cards are saying the situation that started out really negative is going to change into something better. Keep going.

The Anchor/the Bouquet/the Birds/the Mountain/the Coffin

I see this reading as symbolic of a season or era in life coming to an end. The Anchor and Bouquet tell me about a season that was full of accomplishments. The Birds showing up amongst these cards also says it was a season of establishing meaningful connections. But alas, with the Mountain and the Coffin

showing up here, it says this journey in the portion of life is coming to an end. You are seeing situations and relationships coming to an end and life beginning to shift. But remember that every end of a season of life is the beginning of the next. You just have to be willing to let go of things that are familiar to embrace the potential of the future.

The Tower/the Dog/the House/the Sun/the Moon

With the Tower showing up next to the Dog to begin with, this combination represents being faithful to an entity, like a corporation or business. At the same time, the Sun shows up to represent the dawning of a new day but to also reveal the truth, and the Moon says that you need to think deeply about their priorities in life. I see a bit of a workaholic situation being called into contemplation. Are you giving your energy to something that will be worth it in the long run? Look at your work-life balance.

Seven-Card Example Readings

The Bouquet/the Rider/the Woman/the Garden /the Tower/the Fish/the Crossroads

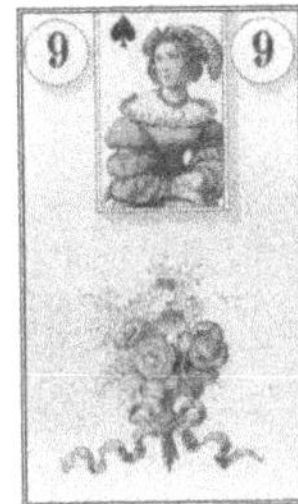

With the appearance of the Bouquet and the Rider as the first two cards, what this tells me is that a new opportunity is heading your way. We know this is a job opportunity because of the Fish, and that Feminine energy will be the bearer of this new lucrative job opportunity, but it would require more from you skills-wise than your current position. The Crossroads tell you that you need to make a decision about the pros and cons of each situation, either staying where you are or making the leap. I think that the extra work would probably be worth it judging from the number of positive cards that show up in this reading. But that's just me!

The Heart/the Bear/the Crossroads/the Book/ the Key/the Moon/the House

I sense this reading, with the Heart and Bear showing up, represents a situation or a person that you love that is not making life easy for you. You have to make a decision (the Crossroads) and reflect on the history you have with this person (the Book). The Key and the Moon tell you to take an honest look at how this situation began and how it's going and base your choice on what is best for you and the peace of your home.

The Letter/the Garden/the Sun/the Moon/ the Coffin/the Heart/the Scythe

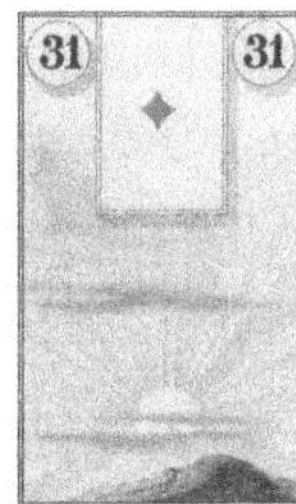

The Letter and the Garden showing up next to each other in this reading represents communication or some kind of correspondence with somebody from your social group that will bring clarity and answers. Those answers will cause you to see certain relationships in situations for what they really are, and the Coffin and Scythe tell you that you need to bring an end to them. It will not feel very good, as you have an emotional attachment to these relationships and they are still near and dear to your heart, but they are not good for you anymore.

More Intricate Spreads

Lenormand isn't limited to just cards in a straight line to tell a story. What follows are some more intricate spreads for Lenormand. These spreads can get very detailed; remember, the more cards that are added to a spread, the more details that are in it. Let's use the sentence *"the dog has fur"* to illustrate this example.

It's a very simple sentence, but we can certainly make it a lot more detailed by adding adjectives. *"The dog has thick black fur."*

But we can give even more detail to our sentence if we add some adverbs. *"The dog with thick black fur was running quickly."*

Again, the more cards we add, the more detailed the reading can be. But one must also know where they stand in their relationship to Spirit and confidence in their reading skills. Large spreads can be very overwhelming to readers who are just starting out, so I recommend waiting until you are comfortable with the card meanings and more familiar with the voice of Spirit before diving into these bigger spreads.

Confidence in connection with Spirit is something that can happen at different times for different people, just like we all learn at different speeds. So, again, don't be discouraged by the size of these spreads. If you put in the practice, you will be as good at reading these spreads as you are at the smaller readings. Remember, divination is like exercising muscles: the more you work it out, the more developed and stronger you will become so you will have the capacity to read bigger spreads like the Petit Tableau or the biggest spread, the Grand Tableau. And, if you're feeling confident enough, you will be able to create your own spread, as you'll see later in the chapter.

Larger spreads such as these come in handy whenever you need all the details of a situation. I myself rarely use the

Tableaus, Grand or Petit, in readings. I wouldn't use them daily; I would stick to the simpler three- and five-card spreads that are illustrated in the previous chapter. But as I stated, these readings will be really good about getting down to brass tacks.

The Petit Tableau

This first complex spread is a good example of one of the only layouts Lenormand is really known for. Where Tarot has the famous Celtic Cross spreads, Lenormand has *Tableaus,* or, in English, "tables." This spread is a miniature version of a spread we will cover next called the Grand Tableau.

The Petit Tableau is a nice layout because you get to see how the cards in a spread are all connected to one another. You'll really start to see for yourself how the card at the beginning of the reading relates to the card at the end. You also get to see how cards meanings can be changed by what cards fall around them. This layout can be read from left to right, but you also need to pay close attention to the cards' positions. If you want a deeper meaning of a certain card in the spread, always look to the card that falls above, behind, in front of, and behind it (if any). I always like to say spreads like this read like a movie story board; you get to see a rough sketch of how the story flows. This layout is really good when you want more detail about a situation but takes a bit longer to interpret. For these reasons, the Petit Tableau is a bit more exhaustive than just normal line reading.

Like I said earlier, the more cards that are included in a single spread, the more detail one can get. When we were reading cards in rows of three, five and seven, I compared them to a sentence in a story. This spread will add even more dimension and detail to your reading, turning it into more of a short story. Whenever I start getting into these spreads, I always make sure I have enough time set aside and I am in a space where I will not be disturbed, as, like I said earlier, these readings can be detail-heavy and exhausting on account of all the cards involved.

Petit Tableau Example Readings

Whenever I start out reading a layout of this size, I always take it one row at a time so as to avoid getting overwhelmed.

The first row, showing the Tower, Ring, and Clouds, is really saying "thunder in paradise." The Tower represents a situation that has been long established, like a job with a company, the Ring represents commitment, and the Clouds represent some uncertainty and trouble that has been cropping up.

The second row, with the Clover, Crossroads, and Rider, says that you are going to come to a crossroads and you will have to make a decision about your future. The rider implies you will have to do it a *lot* sooner than later.

The third row, with the Fox, Anchor, and Bouquet, really says a lot of the rumblings have come from someone who is being very sly and trying to get themselves advanced at the expense of others—and they are just being shady and sneaky in general.

Now, since I have taken it row by row, I start to look at the cards in the reading as a whole and what proximity they have to each other. The Tower showing up in close proximity to the Clover says that you will have to have a degree of cunning to negotiate this situation because the person you're dealing with isn't better by very forthcoming about their intentions and plans.

One of the first things you'll notice about my interpretation, as I stated earlier, is that I take it row by row. I look and see how all the cards in the row work together, then look at how the cards interact with other rows. I am going to go back to my analogy of a Lenormand reading flowing like a book, where a single card can represent a word or a phrase, but a whole row is comparable to a sentence, and the whole reading (in this layout, anyways) is comparable to a short story.

Let's do another Petit Tableau just so we can get an even clearer picture of how to understand it. I am going to pull one more, then let you have a turn to interpret it.

The Stork and the Child represent a new beginning that, with the Whip's appearance, is pretty rough. The Fish and the House say this new beginning transcends just one area of your life and it is affecting your professional life *and* your private life. The fact that the Stork is located so closely to the Fish suggests that the new beginning is a result of new employment that will require you to draw from past experiences and accumulated knowledge. With the last row, the Scythe represents that you were separated and left a familiar and comfortable situation, and the Masculine card there says you also left a love interest to begin this new journey. It will be better for you in the long run.

I handled this reading the same way I handled the previous one: I took it card by card and row by row. On my second pass through, I looked at what cards were near each other. The Stork showing up above the Fish says that the new beginning was brought on by a new employment situation, and the Fish being below the Stork that really underscores the swiftness and possibly the sting of the situation. The initial pass-through is the basic reading, and the second pass, when you are looking at the proximity of the cards, is where the deeper details really come from. I know this all seems rather intimidating at first, but I have full confidence that with practice, you'll be reading cards in no time. Have a little faith in yourself!

The Grand Tableau

This spread is *the* most iconic spread in Lenormand. The Grand Tableau is a spread that is known the world over. It ranks in fame on the same level as the Celtic Cross for Tarot. Did I also mention that it is a massive spread? It uses every single card in the deck! The Grand Tableau is a very deep and very exhaustive reading, chock full of details and depth that, honestly, you would be hard-pressed to find in other systems of divination. In my experience, this reading takes a very long time to finish, and you better write your findings in a journal (if you have not already!). I only do this reading once a year, at New Year's, to give me an outlook on the year ahead, what messages the spirits have for me, and a bit of insight into the coming year.

Example Grand Tableau Reading

You can interpret this reading as each row representing an aspect in life (love, career, home life, etc.) or it can be read from left to right, starting on row one and working your way over. I prefer the latter method because it keeps everything open to what the spirit of the cards has to say. But, without further ado, let's read these cards!

Row One: The Ship showing up so close to the Mice and the Crossroads says there will be an abrupt change. The Crossroads showing up next to the Bear also says this change is going to be a bit rough; you will wrestle with these changes. You'll see an ending in your personal relationships, but don't worry. The Sun says that it will dawn again, and the ending will also reveal people and situations for what they truly are. You should treat them accordingly from that point on. The Whip rounding out this row says these changes and revelations will be pretty painful to deal with. The presence of the Mice, Bear, Coffin, and Whip (four negative heavy-hitters in this context) also really lend themselves to this interpretation as well.

Row Two: The Key showing up first in this row plays well with the previous row that had a lot of endings in it. Because the Key represents a new door opening up for you, alongside its placement next to the Park, it represents being social and making positive connections as well. You will drop your anchor somewhere that is better for you and begin a new journey that the Fox tells you will require a bit of cunning and resourcefulness, but with the Tree rounding out this row, it represents you putting your roots down and doing a lot of growth. The first row talks about the painful aspects of that growth, but with the tree showing up here, this is an aspect of growth where you bear fruit. The Flowers tell me that you will have a reason to celebrate something really big this year.

Row Three: With the Ring and the Rider showing up side-by-side, I see new commitments riding into your life. The Child and Moon represent that this will take you into a new beginning that will draw heavily on the use of intuition, and the Stars represent the need for you to stick to your guns. With the appearance of the Fish, I feel the changes being mentioned here will have to do with job and finances, and a masculine person who is going to herald this will be from a very well-established organization (the Tower).

Row Four: With the Scythe starting out this row next to the Birds, these cards say that there will be a swift separation in your social relationships, but a very educated feminine person will help you through the beginning of this new chapter in life. The Clover and the Lily say this season of life and the connections you are making here will set you down a more positive path in your life. With this new path, you'll be signing your name on the dotted line and taking on new responsibilities, according to the Letter and the Cross.

Row Five: The Stork and the Snake showing up side-by-side say this new season will tell you to use caution when you start diving into new relationships or situations. There will be a bit of uncertainty when it comes to love and relationships, according to the Clouds and the Heart.

I choose to keep this reading brief, but you can add even more detail to this reading when you factor in the cards depending on where they fall in perspective to each other. The cards above and below affect the meaning of cards as much as the cards that fall in front of or behind.

Le Gâteau Spread

This spread is of my own design, and I have been working on perfecting it over my many years of reading. I have never shared it before with anyone. I hope you will find as much of a connection with it as I have. The reason I call it *Le Gâteau,* meaning "the cake," is because it physically resembles a wedding cake. This spread contains two tables of six cards on the bottom, one more table of six above that, then the cake topper, which contains five cards in a cross pattern touching the last table of six. The topper is what I like to call the "take away" cards. It puts the reading in a nutshell for the client so they won't have to stop and muse, "Now what did that card reader say?"

Example Le Gâteau Spread

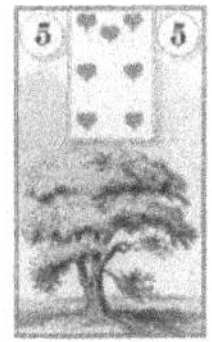

This first table is what I call "the table of the past." What I can see from the Stars, Whip, and Rider showing up side-by-side represents you being in a pretty tough season of change and having to navigate though it. You learned some hard truths and saw some changes in close or familial relationships (represented by the House), while the Tree showing and rounding this portion out says this discomfort brought growth—not at the speed nor in the way you like, but growth is still growth.

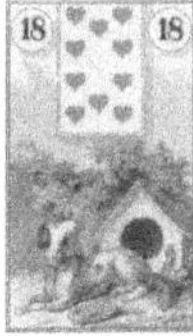

The second table is what I consider the table of the present. The Man starting off this table next to the Stork says a masculine energy is bringing new relationships into your life that will be beneficial. Trust your judgement with some of these new relationships, as there will be some that can talk a big game but are not being completely honest with their words. The Scythe is asking you if you are ready for the changes you are about to experience.

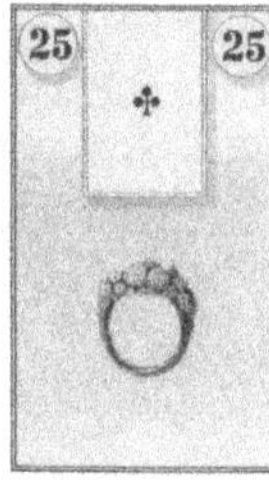

The takeaway cards, also known as the "cross cards," represent the summation of the reading. If you can't remember the whole reading, these cards should be able to give you a "nutshell" synopsis.

I always read this section starting with the middle card. When I pulled these for this example, the Lilies were the card at the center. The takeaway is this season of your life started out pretty crappy, and it will seem like an uphill battle for you with the appearance of the Mountain. Just remember that with the Flowers showing up and pointing the way back to the Lilies card, this season will get better—and it is a season.

You will live more from the heart than you will from the head, so guard your emotions.

In my opinion, this spread can give as much information as the Grand Tableau without having to use the same number of cards. This is the spread I use most frequently, as it is the easiest for me to use and draw information from.

As I have said before, the beauty of Lenormand is that it really has no classical spreads. The closest thing to a "official" spread in Lenormand is the Grand Tableau. A quick Internet search will reveal that people have as many spreads for Lenormand as there are grains of sand on the beach.

As you saw earlier, you have the liberty to experiment and be creative with this process. I created the Le Gâteau spread with a *lot* of experimentation. I tried several different layouts. I worked with each layout to see if it flowed in a way that I could understand. I saw how it felt. That is the key to making your own spread: it can be as simple or as complex as you like, but the big question is, are you understanding the answers it's giving? It's like writing a book. It doesn't even need to make sense to anyone else but you (depending on who you're writing or reading for, anyway). Don't be scared that you will mess up and violate some old universal card reading rule, and that the gods of cartomancy are going to strike you down. Trust me, you won't. Divination has no dogma. So, for your next exercise, create your own spread. experiment. In the words of the beloved teacher and driver of the Magic School Bus, Ms. Frizzle, "Take chances, make mistakes, and get messy!" Now I don't know about the whole messy part, but in my experience, trial and error is the best method for experimentation there is.

This is not an exercise that can be done quickly; it is more of a journey than anything else. Just make sure that, like a scientist, you are journaling your experiences! Write about what works and what didn't. Write about how each layout made you feel. Do you feel like you getting closer to finding "the one" or is it back to the drawing board?

Chapter Six: Lenormand as a Tool for Magical Practice

In my many years of using the cards, I have seen them used and have used them beyond just as tools of divination myself, but also as tools for one's magical practice. It's not a very common practice (much less so than using Tarot in magic), but I have always had great luck with it. This is yet another great example of when I said, "you will get out of this journey what you put into it." Here are a few ways I use Lenormand beyond divination.

Mobile Altar

If you're of the Witchy ilk like me, I always like to bring a little bit of the symbol of connection with me whenever I travel. I have seen this done with Tarot cards before, so this is my adaptation for Lenormand.

Since an altar usually has all of the Elements represented, I use the following cards to represent them.

Earth: The Mountain
For Earth, I use the Mountain card. I can't think of any image that represents this Element better. The

Mountain gives a very grounding energy. It can also represent the path one must follow to make their magic and dreams manifest, as it requires you to walk a path that is sometimes difficult but can be overcame if done with consistency and tenacity.

Air: The Birds or the Scythe

For Air, a card with good imagery would be the Birds or maybe even the Scythe, depending on your thoughts on Elemental alignments. (Some traditions in the past have used the Sword to represent this Element.) The Birds are a pretty good ringer regardless, as they represent a lot of qualities of the Air Element (after all, they, you know…fly).

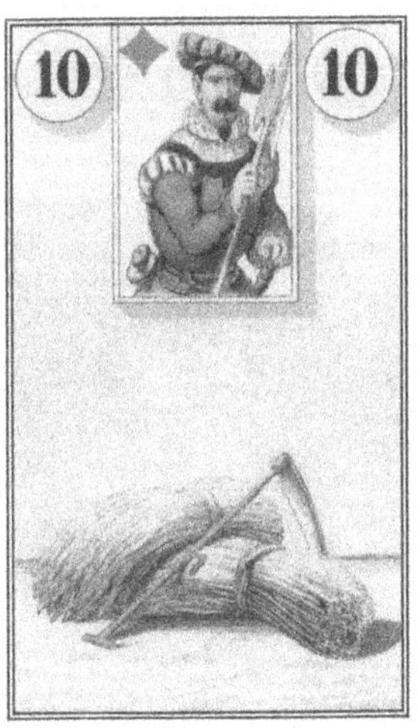

Fire: The Sun

For Fire, the Sun card would be a very good choice, as it represents warmth, illumination, and revealing. Fire also symbolizes passion, focus and the eternal process of destruction and rebirth. Fire also is a symbol for the presence of Spirit.

Water: The Ship

As for the Element of Water, the Ship would work well. Not only is it something that travels on this Element, but it also symbolizes transitions and transformations from one part of life to the next. Just like Fire, Water represents the presence of Spirit, but more so in the aspect of rebirth and cultivation of life.

Spirit: The Key, the Snake, or You

As far as the Element of Spirit goes, there are three choices. I see the Key as a representation, as Spirit is the door from which all Elements sprang forth, so it can symbolize the unlocking of the Elements. Another card would be the Snake. It has been used as a symbol of connection between Heaven (or however you conceive of it) and Earth across time and across various cultures, from Africa, to Europe and the Americas. The third thing that can be used is *you.* You're not a card, but your body is literally a combination of all Elements (blood/water, bones and skin/earth, breath/air, and soul/fire), so your body represents Spirit as it is a house for all Elements.

This mobile altar setup sure beats trying to get an athame through security at the airport! It is also easily concealed whenever you are not in your room. One time, I went on a trip and left my card altar out, and housekeeping wouldn't even clean my room! I think I made them a little concerned, as the front desk clerk was also certainly overly kind after that.

Spell Work with the Cards and a Brief Magical Praxis

Let's begin this section with a question: what exactly *is* magic? My definition of it is but one of a multitude of answers that could be written here. To me, magic is a way energy flows through nature in ways that humanity has not, or will ever be able to, explain. Magic always has and always will be a means for the oppressed to balance the scales. It is a way for those who seemingly have no power to become empowered.

This definition, as with all definitions of magic, is subjective, as the ways we work with the mystical energies of gods, goddesses, spirits, and nature, or anything that has historically been communed with in a spiritual manner, is wide and varied. What you'll find here is but a drop in the bucket. As far as working with any gods, goddesses, or spirits, that isn't a requirement for magic either. I have known some magical folks who choose not to give names of spirits and prefer to interact with the energy of the universe in general.

This leads me to another thing cards can be handy for: if you are of the Witchy ilk, they are great focal points for your spell work! You can use the cards themselves, or you can also use imagery from the cards. One form of spell work with the cards that I find easy to do, as it tends to be cost effective and is very accessible, is candle magic. All you really need is the corresponding color for your intention, your cards, and a *safe* place to burn your candle. You can also use other supplemental things; I have always used finely ground herbs in candles. Herbs can be found tucked away in your spice cabinet at home or on the shelf at your local grocery store. A few other things that you could use are the phase of the Moon, stones, or coins. You do not need to break the bank here. Just like with divination, magic can take any shape.

I always recommend using glass-encased candles that you can find at a lot of Catholic supply stores (if you feel like going undercover!), or you can check and see if your local grocery stores carry them. I am lucky as I live in the Latin district of my city, so I frequent all of the mercados near me, which usually carry glass-encased candles in a ton of colors. Some even come pre-dressed or labeled with a certain intention! The most common ones I see are prosperity, luck, protection, attraction of a lover, and inhibiting of an enemy.

Before we dive into spell work, here is a crash course on one part of my magical philosophy: sometimes negative magic is needed, but it should not be something you reach for first. Should you hex Rhonda in accounting for eating your pudding cup in the office fridge? As much as I love chocolate pudding cups and would tell you blast them into the middle of next week, no...that is *not* a good reason. Is there someone causing harm to your friends or family —or *you*—and you have gone through all the proper channels to try and get them to stop? Then yes, I believe hexes and curses are very necessary in these moments. There are those in the magical community who try to avoid the use of hexes and curses at all costs and let the universe take care of it Sometimes we are called to be the universes' way of "taking care of it." Negative magic or baneful magic is another tool that will always be in the Witch's toolbox. But know this: negative magic has a cost, about 98% or 99% of the time. Another way of putting it is, "Will the payout be worth the cost?" Always measure it against these questions: "Is this necessary? Is this a danger to me, my family or the community?" I believe, in instances where one's safety, health, and mental health is at stake, there isn't a cost. Like I said earlier, sometimes *we* are the universe's tool for "taking care of it." I have been in situations where I have worked baneful magick to protect myself, my family and my community. However, I will not be including any hexes or curses here. Maybe another book? I think this statement is best summed up by a quote by Theodore Rosevelt, "Speak softly and carry a big stick; you will go far," meaning that you should always strive to be peaceful, but have the ability to take care of things if the situation go sideways.

Another bit of safety housekeeping: please burn your candles somewhere safe, and make sure you extinguish the candle before you leave the house. Don't worry about the spell still working if the candle is not lit. As long as you don't blow the candle out, you're good! You can use a candle snuffer (there are some pretty cool ones out there!), a metal lid from a jar, or the lid of your cauldron if you have one. The reason I specify not to blow it out is that, not only does it show a difference between just burning a regular candle, it also comes from the belief about "blowing the magic away."

Where to Start

I always begin any magical work with grounding and centering. This helps to get your intention set and, to quote various other practitioners, get into "the magical mindset." Preparing yourself will also help you hash out the intention and purpose of the work. Speaking of intention, every great magical working should begin with crystal clear intention. Always ask yourself who, what, and why. Who am I doing this for? Myself, a friend, family, or someone else? What is my (or their) situation? What steps have been taken to get the desired results from mundane channels? Why am I doing this work? Why is this situation happening? Questions like this are why it is important to have something like a journal to record your readings and spell work. Writing out the answers to these questions tends to help you hash out all those answers and revise if needed.

Some other things that can add a little oomph to your work could be to use the phases of the Moon, such as using the waning moon to reduce the influence or strength of something, the waxing moon to make something grow and multiply, or the full moon, which is pretty all-encompassing and has all the spiritual properties of waxing and waning phases. I do not do this personally, but days of the week are also often associated with different magical needs, like Monday for doing work to remove obstacles, Tuesday for protection magic, and Friday for attraction of good luck, money, or love.

You'll notice that I include "optional" items in these spells; these are things that can be used to heighten or add a bit more flavor to a working. They are not requirements. Some people would have an issue waiting for the right moon phase, or the crystal or herbs I mention might fall outside the budget this month. That's okay! (A lot of the herbs I use here are very accessible.) It may also be helpful to buy a conventional deck of cards to use for a given spell. Spell work can be very messy, and you do not want to ruin a card deck you love with candle wax.

The next thing that helps spell work is to have a space that is charged and set. Sometimes this has been referred to as casting a circle. Casting a circle or creating a sacred space makes a space outside of time and reality as we know it, also known as a *liminal space.* The exercise I gave earlier in this book—the circle of sound, light, and smoke on page 90—should fit the bill to cast a circle just fine. Or you can look up the multitude of other ways folks have done it. This has been historically done with salt, chalk, or cornmeal, or drawing a circle with a stang, wand, or broom. I have personally used dragon's blood incense sticks, a pair of scissors, and my index finger. You can use almost anything to demarcate the working space.

In the following exercise, I will share another method I have used to cast a circle in my personal practice.

Alternative Circle Casting Exercise

Begin by entering a meditative state via the methods I've named earlier in this book or any way that makes you comfortable and calms your mind.

Take a nice, slow, deep breath and, on the exhale, imagine a root coming down from your feet and pushing deep into the earth.

Take three more of those nice deep breaths. With each inhale, imagine you are drawing up a grounding red energy into your body via the soles of your feet. Feel it seeping into your bones. How does it feel? Does it feel cool and moist, like soil under your feet? Is it warming? Does it feel heavy or light?

When you feel ready, take three more deep breaths and imagine branches beginning to slowly grow from your shoulders and the crown of your head. The branches get bigger and higher with each breath. Your limbs and branches have grown so tall that the very stars and planets are trapped in your limbs. Now, begin to breathe in the energy of the sky, down through your branches into your crown. How does it feel? Is it lighter than the earthen energy, or do you feel the weight of the sky on your shoulders?

Letting both energies flow in you, take a moment and let the feelings of earth and sky merge in your solar plexus. At the point where they meet, imagine a white ball beginning to grow. With each breath, the ball gets bigger. Once you feel the ball has reached an appropriate size, put your hands on your stomach and will the ball from your stomach up through your throat. Let it float out from your hand to whatever distance you want your working space to be.

Begin moving in a clockwise direction, seeing the ball following your finger and leaving a white light trail. Once you reach your starting point again, visualize yourself encircled by a warm white light.

This method helps when you don't have access to any tools and need to do some work in a hurry!

Here are a few spells you can do with your Lenormand deck.

The Sun Truth Card

- Yellow or white candle
- Sun card
- A piece of paper
- Optional crystal: sunstone or quartz crystal
- Optional herbs: sunflower seeds, basil, or angelica

The purpose of this work is to get to the truth of a situation using the energy of the Sun card in its capacity as a revealer of truth. This spell is helpful when you sense someone isn't quite being fully honest.

Start by writing the name of the person who isn't quite being honest on a piece of paper five or seven times, then cross your writing with the phrase "tell me the truth!"

Then, fold the paper away from you three times and put it under the candle. Either add a few drops of the herbs if they are in oil, or grind them down into a powder and sprinkle them on the top of the candle.

Any time of day will work for this spell, but it works best on sunrise on a Sunday.

Cut and Clear Scythe Spell

- Black candle
- Scythe card
- Piece of paper
- Optional herbs: wormwood, sage, or lemon rind
- Optional moon phase: the waning moon

This spell is handy when you are trying to cut an influence from your life, be it a person or a situation that is not good for you or your community. It's pretty simple to set up.

Take your name paper and write the name of the situation or person you want to be rid of. Do so seven times vertically, then turn the paper and write it again seven times, crossing the first set you wrote horizontally. Fold the paper three times away from you, then place it under the candle, or, if you want to add another layer of protection, you can choose to burn your candle on a coaster made of glass or stone, placing the name paper under it all.

Say a prayer or a statement of intention (you could even say what you wrote on the paper out loud).

Gently knock the candle on the table or the surface next to the candle, then light it. (This knocking is to "wake up" the candle.)

Let the candle burn for as long as you like, but please put it out before you leave your home or go to bed for the night. You can do this by either using a traditional candle snuffer or putting something like a plate or cup (ceramic, stone, glass, or metal only!) over the top. This will cut off oxygen to the flame and it will gently go out.

When you are ready to light it again, just repeat the same process! Make sure you journal this process, too. Do you notice any differences? Is the situation lessening?

Prosperity Fish Card Spell

In a pinch and need some quick cash? Looking to get into a better financial situation in life? This is the spell for you! If you recall from the card guide in Chapter Two, the Fish symbolizes money, income, and wealth. Here's what you'll need:

- A gold or green candle (some places offer combos of the two colors in the same candle)
- Fish card
- A piece of paper
- Optional herbs: cinnamon, basil, or Solomon's seal
- Optional crystals: quartz, malachite, or pyrite and coins of varying values
- Optional moon phase: a waxing or full moon

Repeat the same process as the Cut and Clear Scythe spell, but instead of writing something on the paper to be cut and clear you of someone or something, write something about prosperity or wealth finding you. For example, you could write "money will find me very soon!" seven times, then turn the paper and write the phrase again seven times, crossing your first. Then fold it three times towards you. There are some good herbs I have had luck with for this type of work, especially dried hot peppers, like guinea pepper (also called Grains of Paradise), red pepper, or jalapeno pepper.

Everything's Coming Up Lily Spell

This spell is based on the transformative energy that the Lily card poses. It is spell that can turn situations from shit to flowers. What you'll need is:

- A white candle
- Lily card
- A piece of paper

I like to keep this work very simple. If you are already dealing with a crazy situation, the last thing you want to have to look for is the appropriate stone or herb, or worry what phase the Moon is in.

Follow the same process listed in the spells using the Fish and Scythe cards, writing your intentions on the paper as something like "this will turn around in my favor." Like before, write it seven times. Turn the paper and write your intention again, crossing the first set of words. Fold the paper toward you and knock as described earlier. Extinguish as needed.

The possibilities are endless when it comes to this spell. This basic framework I have given above can be used for almost any type of magical ends (love, luck, protection, etc.).

If you choose to use the optional herbs, you can either use them in the form of an essential oil, or the dried herbs themselves if they are pulverized down into a fine powder where they will not clog the wick or catch fire easily.

Ethics and Mindsets

To wrap up this adventure, allow me to offer you a few pointers on the dos and don'ts of doing readings for other folks, should you decide to venture that way. But these tips will also help keep you on the straight and narrow when it comes to being any type of reader. There are also a few traits to cultivate that will help you grow as a reader that relate.

Honesty

I know I've mentioned this here and there, but I cannot overstate the importance of developing the ability to be honest with yourself when reading for yourself. At the end of the day, the truth that comes out in the cards is the truth you need to see. It doesn't matter whether you acknowledge it or not.

Remember, the future revealed in the cards is the path you are on, but don't forget the future is fluid. On an added note, this quality will come in handy if you decide to read for others as well. Honesty is the best policy.

Persistence and Patience

Another important point is to be persistent in your work and patient with yourself. Like I said earlier, everyone has to start at some point and build from there, but you *must* follow through with your practice. You will get out of this path what you put into it. Only with practice over time will you gain confidence and learn to distinguish the voice of the spirits and the voices that try to lead you away.

Curiosity

I am sure by now you've heard the adage, "Curiosity killed the cat!" But curiosity is also a good trait to maintain as a reader, because it is the fuel to drive you deeper into your path. It is the lure that Spirit uses to draw out your creativity and question whether the boundaries we have created for ourselves are made out of fear or safety. Never let the childlike trait of asking "why" fade from your soul. I could dive into the concept of engaging your inner child, but that would be a whole book unto itself.

Humility

One trait that is very important to have as a reader is a sense of humility and gratitude. Humility is not about downplaying your abilities but is about not puffing yourself up. It's knowing that your abilities speak for themselves and not needing to doctor them up with lots of flash and big talk. Humility is the *knowing* you have what it takes but not *needing* to brag about it or put down others. It is about remembering where you came from and knowing what it was like to begin.

Reading cards doesn't make you better than anyone else. If anything, it should mean you have a greater sense of responsibility for the choices that you make in our daily lives and accepting the call for change when it is needed. Humility is being able to hold the mirror of change to our faces and then making those changes reality. I speak from personal experience on this one: Lenormand has read me for filth numerous times, not to put me down and step on me, but to help me do better in life in general.

Gratitude

Gratitude is showing appreciation for the relationship you have with Spirit, being grateful for the connection one has to Spirit, and the ability to be able to understand and act on it with confidence. Gratitude is being grateful we didn't throw in the towel and walk away from a rich—and occasionally difficult—connection with the spirits and also knowing that this relationship is not one many get to have in their lives. Gratitude for this connection is something that is lived, not just spoken. I think this quote by former president John F. Kennedy is a pretty good way to sum this up: "As we express our gratitude, we must never forget that the highest appreciation is not to utter words, but to live by them."

The traits I have listed above are, at the end of the day, just advice. As with all advice, you are welcome to take it or leave it. But as card readers I believe in always having a moral compass that points to the north. With all the stereotypes we have to deal with in the world, unfortunately I believe we do not have the option to even have the slightest hint of deception or duplicity. When you have an uncommon connection, it's normal to have uncommon values. What is sad is the fact that these *are* uncommon values.

Conclusion

I am so happy I've had the opportunity to share this path I have been walking and loving for many years. I hope this book serves as a launching pad for you to dive into the mysteries that Lenormand has to offer, giving you insight, direction, and confidence. The cards will take care of you if you venture to get to know them. Happy card slinging.

—E. M.

Bibliography

Anonymous. "Mademoiselle Lenormand, the Fortune Teller." *Remarkable Women of Different Nations and Ages.* John P. Jewett and Company, 1858.

Dos Ventos, Mario. *The Game of Destiny - Fortune Telling with Lenormand Cards.* Nzo Quimbanda Exu Ventania, 2007.

Layla the Lenormand Reader. "The Game of Hope." *Lenormand Reader,* 22 June 2022, www.lenormandreader.com/blog/the-game-of-hope.

Lenormand, Marie Anne. *Historical and Secret Memoirs of the Empress Josephine (Marie Rose Tascher De La Pagerie), First Wife of Napoleon Bonaparte.* Forgotten Books, 2018.

—. *The Prophetic Memories of a Sibyl on the Secret Causes of her Arrest.* 1814.